pretty little mini quilts

pretty little mini quilts

LARK BOOKS

A Division of Sterling Publishing Co., Inc.
New York / London

SENIOR EDITOR
Ray Hemachandra

EDITOR
Larry Shea

ART DIRECTOR
Megan Kirby

ART PRODUCTION
Jeff Hamilton

ILLUSTRATOR
Susan McBride

PHOTOGRAPHERS
Steve Mann
Stewart O'Shields

COVER DESIGNER
Celia Naranjo

Library of Congress Cataloging-in-Publication Data

Pretty little mini quilts / editor, Ray Hemachandra. -- 1st ed.
    p. cm.
  Includes index.
  ISBN 978-1-60059-493-9 (hc-plc with jacket : alk. paper)
  1. Patchwork--Patterns. 2. Quilting--Patterns. 3. Miniature quilts.
  TT835.P698 2010
  746.46'041--dc22

                                   2009034457

10 9 8 7 6 5 4 3 2 1

First Edition

Published by Lark Books, A Division of
Sterling Publishing Co., Inc.
387 Park Avenue South, New York, NY 10016

Text © 2010, Lark Books, A Division of Sterling Publishing Co., Inc.
Photography © 2010, Lark Books, A Division of Sterling Publishing Co., Inc.
Illustrations © 2010, Lark Books, A Division of Sterling Publishing Co., Inc.

Distributed in Canada by Sterling Publishing,
c/o Canadian Manda Group, 165 Dufferin Street
Toronto, Ontario, Canada M6K 3H6

Distributed in the United Kingdom by GMC Distribution Services,
Castle Place, 166 High Street, Lewes, East Sussex, England BN7 1XU

Distributed in Australia by Capricorn Link (Australia) Pty Ltd.,
P.O. Box 704, Windsor, NSW 2756 Australia

If you have questions or comments about this book, please contact:
Lark Books, 67 Broadway, Asheville, NC 28801, 828-253-0467

Manufactured in China

ISBN 13: 978-1-60059-493-9

For information about custom editions, special sales, and premium and corporate purchases, please contact the Sterling Special Sales Department at 800-805-5489 or specialsales@sterlingpub.com.

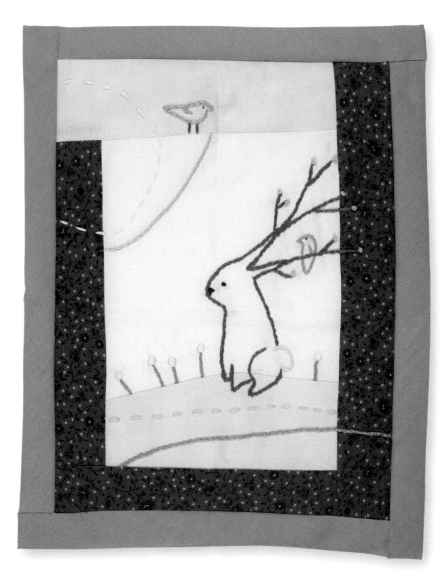

contents

introduction

What's the most traditional sewing you can do? Making quilts, of course. The word itself calls up thoughts of a quilting bee near that little house on the prairie, or of that cozy Log Cabin quilt your grandmother handed down to you (or the one you wish she had). Unless you're stitching up petticoats, nothing you're sewing has stronger ties to the past than quilts.

What's the most contemporary, cutting-edge (pun intended) sewing you can do? Same answer. With the explosion of art quilts being created today—abstract, figurative, collage, and more—you're now more likely to see a quilt in a gallery or museum than on a four-poster bed.

Welcome to the best of both worlds. Come along as more than two dozen talented designers create 31 mini quilts that look to the past as they rush forward to a fresh future. You'll find quilts like *Checkered Past* (page 45) and *Bright Teeth* (page 63) that use traditional quilting motifs in works of modern abstraction. Charming scenes like *Days of Summer* (page 40) and *Yard Tale* (page 66) could come from a folk-art collection or a child's drawing on the fridge. *Portrait of Velma* (page 77) employs imaging software and a scanner to create a loving picture of the designer's grandmother. And *Dress Shop Memories* (page 96) is a not-at-all-traditional assemblage that honors seamstresses from decades past.

In *Pretty Little Mini Quilts*, you'll see plenty of projects—both timeless and timely—that you'll love to make. More good news: Unlike many sewn creations that stay hidden in a drawer or closet, quilts can be displayed on the wall in all their "Hey, I made that!" glory. And because these are mini quilts (each measuring no more than 36 inches [91.4 cm] square), you won't need a whole wall to put one up or weeks of sewing before it's finished. How does tomorrow sound?

In this book, you'll find all the detailed instructions and basic information you need for creating great mini quilts. One old quilting tradition is to intentionally break the color pattern for just one square, in the belief that trying to create something absolutely perfect shows too much pride. When making these projects, don't even try to live up to anyone else's idea of perfection. It's not like sewing up a pair of pants, where making one leg longer than the other is usually considered a mistake and not an artistic choice. With these decorative pieces, you get to decide when to closely follow our designers' choices for color and decoration and when to set off on your own path. (In the case of *Through the Labyrinth* on page 134, we mean that literally.) You'll know when a mini quilt is your own version of perfect, ready for the world to admire. Then go ahead and show some pride—you'll have earned it!

pretty little
mini quilts
basics

Whether you're a veteran quilter, or someone with a little sewing experience looking to try something new, mini quilts are fun and easy to make. This chapter provides you with the information you need about tools, materials, and techniques to make all the quilts in this book. If you have a problem making any of the projects, just come back here for a refresher course.

10

quilt tools

Don't worry about having to pony up for special, expensive tools—you can probably find almost all the things you'll need for quilting among your sewing supplies. Use the Basic Quilting Tool Kit as a checklist to make sure you're ready to go. The lists of materials and supplies ("What You Need") in the projects won't include these basic items; they'll just tell you anything special you need for that particular project.

SEWING SCISSORS

If it's time for a new pair of sewing scissors, remember that good quality is worth the extra cost. Give the scissors a test run at the store before purchasing them. If they fit comfortably in your hands, you can look forward to years of happy cutting—as long you use them for fabric only, that is. Using them to cut paper will dull the blades, making them useless on fabric. Once you have a good pair of regular sewing scissors, invest in some fine-tipped scissors, such as embroidery scissors. They're great for working in smaller spaces, making it easy to maneuver when doing tiny detail work.

basic quilting tool kit

- *Sharp sewing scissors (for fabric)*
- *Craft scissors (for paper)*
- *Sewing machine*
- *Sewing machine needles*
- *Hand-sewing needles*
- *Rotary cutter and mat*
- *Measuring tape*
- *Transparent ruler*
- *Tailor's chalk or water-soluble fabric marker*
- *Seam ripper*
- *Iron and ironing board*
- *Needle threader*
- *Straight pins*
- *Safety or basting pins*
- *Thread*
- *Pencil and paper for making templates*

CRAFT SCISSORS

An all-purpose pair of moderate length works well when cutting out curves and corners on paper patterns and templates. Be sure to use them when cutting anything that's not fabric.

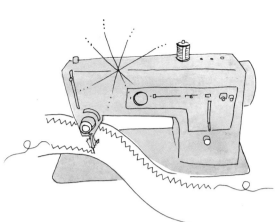

SEWING MACHINE

Yes, you can quilt by hand if you'd like. And, indeed, many of the stitches you'll need for the projects here can only be done that way. But for making quilts (whether mini or maxi), a standard sewing machine is a basic necessity. Machines with special stitching capabilities (like satin, zigzag, or blanket stitches) can even help you fake those hand-stitched details so well that no one will know you didn't spend hours on them yourself (we won't tell).

PRACTICE, PRACTICE

Every sewing machine is different, so check your manual for adjusting stitches. If you're trying out a new setting or stitch, give it a go on a spare piece of fabric before using your carefully cut project pieces.

SEWING MACHINE NEEDLES

Machine needles are inexpensive, and it's good to always have a few packs on hand. You really don't want to see a needle break on a project with no replacement available, especially if you're only a few yards from the finish stitch. Get into the habit of starting each project with a new needle; you'll be glad to have a running start without any pesky needle problems.

HAND-SEWING NEEDLES

A variety pack of needles will do the job for the general sewing in this book. Its range of needle sizes allows you to sew together most common fabrics. Some projects will ask for an embroidery needle, which has a longer eye to accommodate thicker embroidery floss.

ROTARY CUTTER AND MAT

Quilters were among the first to discover how these cutters, with their sharp rolling wheels, quickly slice through multiple layers of fabric. You can use scissors for the same tasks you'd use a rotary cutter for, but it won't be as quick or convenient. The grid on the self-healing mat is especially helpful for lining up and measuring your cuts.

MEASURING TAPE AND TRANSPARENT RULER

For measuring out lengths of fabrics or other materials, a measuring tape can't be beat. But for making small measurements, drawing straight lines, and making sure a quilt square is just the right size, a transparent ruler truly rules. You can also use the ruler as a straight edge when you're using a rotary cutter.

TAILOR'S CHALK AND FABRIC MARKING PENS

When you need to see a marking or line just for now, but not later, these are the tools to use. Use a water-soluble fabric marker to make sewing or cutting lines and embroidery designs. The ink will disappear with plain water. Test a marker first on a scrap of a new fabric, as the dyes in some fabrics can make the ink hard to remove. Tailor's chalk leaves dust on the surface of the fibers, but it's easy to brush the marks away once you don't need them anymore.

SEAM RIPPER

A seam ripper can undo mistakes in no time. Just start over again like nothing bad happened (and, if you think about it, nothing really did).

IRON AND IRONING BOARD

An iron isn't just for getting rid of wrinkles before you sew. This invaluable tool also sets seams and hems, and it applies the heat to fusible web, transfers, and appliqués.

NEEDLE THREADER

Folks with perfect eyesight and rock-steady hands can skip this tool. Otherwise, save yourself some frustration by using a needle threader. Simply push the thin wire loop of this tiny tool through the eye of the needle, insert the thread, and pull the loop out.

STRAIGHT PINS

You can use short metal pins with small heads to do the job, but the longer pins with plastic or glass heads are easier to handle and more fun to look at.

COLOR CODE

Here's one advantage of using straight pins with colored heads: You can use different colors as codes to indicate what to do next. Green means "start stitching here," while red means "stop here." And purple might mean "take a break for a nice cup of tea."

SAFETY OR BASTING PINS

Sew safely, now! When pinning layers in place, safety pins give you fewer sharp points to worry about. Basting pins, with a bend in the arm for reaching through thick quilt layers, are another great invention to be thankful for.

ASSORTED TOOLS

In the "What You Need" section for the projects, a few other tools will pop up occasionally. They include:

GLUE AND ADHESIVES

You can use clear glue instead of stitching to affix a button or add an embellishment. Adhesives are also handy for basting quickly without stitches.

STAPLE GUN AND STAPLES

Use the staples to attach fabric to a frame.

EMBROIDERY HOOP

For a large quilt, you might want to employ one of those quilt frames your grandmother used (or at least could have used). When you need to hold fabric taut in these mini quilts, an embroidery hoop will do the trick. Two simple wooden circles, one inside the other, hold fabric tightly in place as you embroider.

quilt materials

Anyone who's been sewing for a while has a stash of fabrics, notions, and embellishments on hand, including some scraps and odds and ends you have no idea what to do with. The great thing about quilting is this: With a little creativity, you can find a purpose for just about all of them. An even greater thing: You can still go out to the fabric or craft store to buy some more.

THREADS

A quality polyester thread is your best choice for all-purpose machine and hand sewing. In most cases, an average all-purpose thread, usually a cotton/polyester blend, will do fine too. Some quilts in this book call for quilting thread, which is slightly finer and stronger than all-purpose thread. If you want your quilting stitches to blend in with the background, pick a color that matches your main fabrics. A clear nylon thread will just about disappear. On the other hand, if you want a contrasting color for design purposes (or you just want to show off all the stitches you've done), select threads in bold, contrasting colors.

EMBROIDERY FLOSSES

A number of projects include a touch of embroidery as an embellishment. Use multi-strand embroidery floss in cotton, silk, or rayon to add these decorative highlights.

FUSIBLE WEB

This no-sew alternative for affixing fabric to fabric is fantastic for making appliqués, and it's pretty great for other purposes too. Fusible web uses a heat-activated adhesive to become sticky. Paper-backed fusible web, similar to double-sided tape, lets you adhere two surfaces together.

INTERFACING

Interfacing can add more support and structure to your projects. It comes in different weights, but it's best to use light- or medium-weight interfacing for subtle shaping. Fusible interfacing, applied with an iron, works well on most fabrics.

LAYERING MATERIALS

In the quilt "sandwich," the quilt top gets all the publicity. The quilt backing is an underrated performer that occasionally gets its due, especially on more reversible quilts. But it's the layering material in the middle, usually called batting, that works in obscurity to turn two pieces of cloth into something warm, fluffy, and cozy.

ANY SIZE YOU LIKE

If you can't find batting that's as wide or as long as your quilt, don't worry. Using a simple zigzag stitch along the edges (which no one will ever see), you can easily join pieces of batting to make the size you need.

Batting is available in various materials from cotton to blends to polyester. If you may eventually wash your quilt, know that polyester and polyester blends can usually survive a gentle machine wash and tumble dry while cotton batting cannot. You can choose different thicknesses as well. Low-loft batting is thinner, easier to sew through, and great for a quilt with a lot of detail. High-loft batting is warmer and puffier, but it may make it harder to see any hand-stitched elements.

You can buy batting at most fabric stores in a variety of widths right off the bolt, like fabric, or in precut sizes. Keep in mind that your batting will need to be a few inches longer and wider than your quilt top.

RIBBONS, RICKRACK, AND TRIMS

Whether in grosgrain, satin, or velvet, ribbon provides a great decorative touch. A bit of lace trim can add a touch of elegance or whimsy. Rickrack, that wavy favorite, makes for a fun way to add detail to designs or to finish edges, as in the Corner Store quilt on page 51.

BUTTONS, EYELETS, AND SNAPS

Remember when we said above that you could use just about anything in your sewing stash on a quilt? Buttons and other fasteners usually have a job to do on sewn objects, but with a quilt there's just one question to ask: Does it look cool? Yes? Then sew it on.

BIAS TAPE

Bias tape is made from strips of fabric cut on the bias (diagonal) rather than the straight of the grain. This allows the perfect amount of stretch for skirting corners and curves when binding raw edges. You can purchase single-fold or double-fold bias tape in various widths. We'll talk a lot more about binding later on in the Techniques section.

FABRICS

For a quilter, walking into a fabric store can be a dizzying experience. So many possibilities, and so many ways to combine them! When you consider the choices of material, weight, color, and pattern, it's hard to know where to turn. Here are a few things to keep in mind before your shopping cart gets filled to the top.

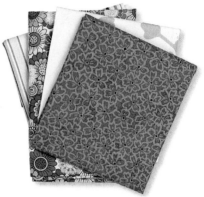

COTTON

Simple cotton is the most popular and versatile fabric around. Medium-weight cotton is suitable for making most of the quilts in this book. It's easy to sew, holds up well, and comes in a wide variety of colors and patterns. In most cases, you'll need to pre-wash your fabric to avoid any later problems with color bleeding or shrinkage.

FELT

What's not to love about felt? It's soft, doesn't ravel, has no right or wrong side, and you can buy it in just about any store that carries sewing or craft supplies. Traditionally, felt is made of wool, although the squares or bolts of felt you find in stores may be made from synthetic fibers.

LINEN

Linen (most often preceded by the word "crisp") is a good choice when you need a durable fabric with a bit of body to it. Linen does wrinkle, so iron it often before, during, and after sewing to keep it smooth.

FLEECE

Fleece is durable and easy to sew, as well as washable and quick-drying. Its main draw, though, is its inviting plush texture.

SILK

Silk (frequently preceded by the word "luxurious") adds refinement to any quilt. Silk is sturdier than it looks, but choose medium- to heavyweight silk to stand up to use.

WOOL

Wool is a classic sewing fabric that adds texture and charm to any quilt. Find old wool suits or coats and give a piece of their fabric a new life.

PLAYING WITH QUARTERS

A fat quarter is a half yard of fabric that has been cut in half to make a piece measuring 18 x 21 inches (45.7 x 53.3 cm). Fat quarters are big enough to add the right touch to a quilt, and small enough to keep a big variety on hand for just the shade or pattern you need to fill out that quilt corner.

quilt techniques

Putting together a quilt is just like putting together a sandwich. Take a look at figure 1: You put down your backing (the first slice of bread), then your batting (the filling), and cover it with your quilt top (the other slice of bread). No problem! Okay, maybe assembling a quilt is actually a little more complicated than slapping together a tuna salad on wheat. But reading the tips, tricks, and techniques in this section will give you the knowledge you need to create your own fabric masterpieces.

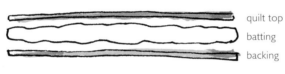

quilt top
batting
backing

figure 1

CUTTING

Let's back up a step for a second. Before taking scissors to fabric, your first move is usually to wash your fabrics, using the same settings you'd use when laundering the finished quilt. This will avoid any problems later with shrinkage or running colors. If your fabric gets super wrinkly in the wash, give it a quick pressing.

When it's time to cut your pieces to size, remember that you'll need to add about ¼ inch (6 mm) to each edge to accommodate the seam allowance, unless the instructions tell you not to add any allowance, or the materials list gives you an exact size to cut to. You can cut all your pieces before you start or cut them along the way, but be sure to keep your pieces organized and even labeled, if that helps avoid confusion.

A PERFECT CUT

When cutting with a rotary cutter and mat, follow these steps for a straight and safe cut. Hold the cutter at a 45° angle, with the blade firmly against the ruler's edge. Keep even pressure on the cutter, and always cut away from yourself. Keep the safety latch on when the cutter is not in use, and replace blades as needed.

MACHINE STITCHING

Unless you like to quilt when you're out and about (and have a lot of free time), most of the stitches in your mini quilts will probably be machine stitches. Before you begin, test the tension of your machine by stitching on a scrap of the fabric you'll be using. If necessary, follow the instructions in your machine's manual to adjust the tension for the top thread or the bobbin. Then follow these steps to sew the perfect seam.

1 Pin the fabric pieces together, using straight pins placed at right angles to the seam. Unless the project instructions tell you otherwise, most seams are sewn with right sides together and raw edges aligned.

2 As you sew, pull the pins out before they reach the needle. Be quick! If you're too late, the machine needle can nick the pins, which will dull or even break the needle.

3 To make a sharp angle for a corner, you need to pivot the fabric. When you get to the corner point, stop with the needle down in the fabric. Then lift the presser foot, turn the fabric, lower the presser foot, and keep on sewing.

4 Let the machine do the work of pulling the fabric through as you sew. This will save you uneven stitches, stretched fabric, puckered seams, and a lot of wasted energy.

5 Pay attention to those seam allowances, knowing that ¼ inch (6 mm) is pretty standard (figure 2). Use the measurement lines on the throat plate as a guide while you feed the fabric along.

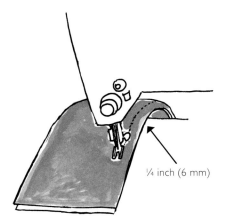

¼ inch (6 mm)

figure 2

HAND STITCHES

Sometimes you have to put aside your machine and take up needle and thread (or floss). Here are the most common stitches you'll need for the projects in this book.

APPLIQUÉ STITCH

Done right, these tiny stitches are practically invisible. Use them when stitching on an appliqué. Poke the needle through the base fabric and up through the appliqué. Bring the needle down into the base fabric just a bit away and repeat.

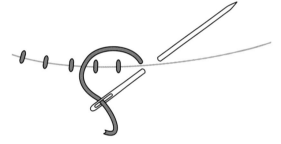

BACKSTITCH

The backstitch is a basic method for creating a seam that works well for holding seams under pressure. It can also be used to outline shapes or text.

BLANKET STITCH

The blanket stitch is both decorative and functional. Use this stitch to accentuate an edge or to attach an appliqué.

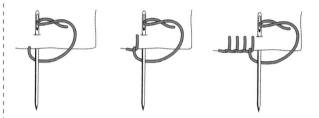

FRENCH KNOT

This elegant little knot adds interest and texture when embroidering or embellishing.

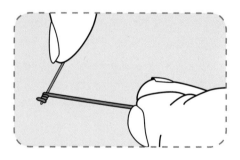

RUNNING STITCH

Make this stitch by weaving the needle through the fabric at evenly spaced intervals.

SLIPSTITCH

This stitch is perfect for closing seams. Slip the needle through one end of the open seam to anchor the thread, and then take a small stitch through the fold, pulling the needle through. In the other side of the seam, insert the needle directly opposite the stitch you just made, and take a stitch through the fold. Repeat.

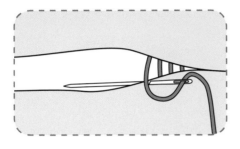

WHIPSTITCH

The whipstitch is used to bind two edges together. Sew the stitches over the edge of the fabric.

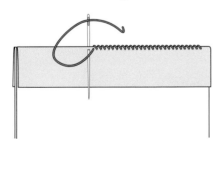

CLIPPING CORNERS AND CURVES

When you turn a quilt right side out (as you sometimes will), any excess fabric can bunch in the seams. Don't worry, though. A few well-placed snips and clips can prevent any lumps and bumps in your work.

After sewing, cut the seam allowance at a 45° angle to the raw edge. Cut close to the stitching, but be careful to avoid cutting the stitches (figure 3).

figure 3

Sewn curves are a little different. You clip an inward curve but notch an outward one. To clip an inward curve, cut into the seam allowance at several places around the curve (figure 4). Don't clip too close, since you don't want to cut into the stitching. To notch an outward curve, cut small V-shaped wedges from the seam allowance (figure 5), also making sure you don't cut into the stitching.

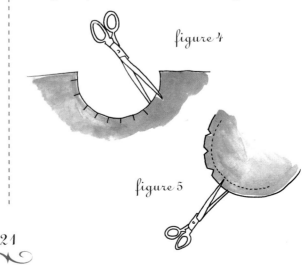

figure 4

figure 5

PIECING

A few quilts in this book have one main piece for the quilt top, with decorative elements such as appliqué or embroidery added on top of it. Most quilts, though, require some amount of piecing, a process used in traditional quilts. True to its name, piecing involves small pieces being sewn together into larger units, and eventually into the entire quilt design.

A sewing machine is best for piecing, though piecing by hand is also possible. Here's how to do it.

1 Lay two pieces of fabric together with right sides facing.

2 Pin the pieces together along the edge where they will be joined.

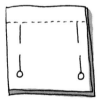

3 Straight stitch along the side, about ¼ inch (6 mm) in from the raw edge of the fabric (figure 6).

figure 6

4 Lay the pieces out flat, and, using an iron, press the seams to one side (making them lie under the darker fabric, if possible) or open, depending on the instructions (figure 7).

figure 7

ATTACHING A BORDER

Some quilts use borders to frame the central design. As in piecing, you'll attach a border using a ¼-inch (6 mm) seam allowance (unless directed otherwise) and then iron the seams to one side.

1 Cut fabric strips in the correct dimensions for each border of the quilt.

2 Working first on a short side of the quilt, pin the border strip to the quilt top with right sides together (figure 8).

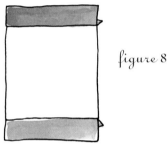

figure 8

3 Stitch along the edge, using a ¼-inch (6 mm) seam allowance. Press the seam out toward the border. Repeat steps 2 and 3 for the quilt's other short side, then for the two long sides (figure 9).

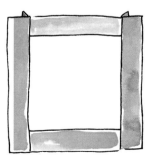

figure 9

ATTACHING APPLIQUÉS

Adding fabric cutouts is a great way to quickly add texture and visual interest to a quilt. You can sew them on by hand or machine. One of the quickest ways to apply appliqués is to use lightweight paper-backed fusible web to fix them to the fabric.

1 Apply the fusible web to the fabric following the manufacturer's instructions. Do not remove the paper backing. Draw or trace the outline of the appliqué directly on the paper, then cut it out. (Because you're working on the wrong side of the fabric, the design you draw will appear in reverse when you apply it.)

2 Remove the paper backing. Position the appliqué on your fabric, and press it with an iron according to the instructions.

3 You can finish the edges of the appliqué to keep them from raveling by using either a hand or machine stitch. Applying fray retardant before affixing the appliqué will also help prevent raveling.

EMBROIDERY

Embroidery is another technique that allows you to add an artistic design to your quilt canvas (literally or figuratively). Embroidery stitches are more decorative than those for appliqué, as you're not attaching fabric to fabric. You're simply making decorative stitches through a layer of fabric.

If an embroidery pattern is a simple one (and you're pretty confident about your drawing skills), you can copy it by hand with a fabric marker or pencil before stitching. Otherwise, you can directly transfer the pattern to your piece of fabric. For light fabrics you can see through, lay the fabric over the design and trace it with a sharp pencil or fabric marker. For darker fabrics, transfer the design by using a light box (or taping it to a window) or using fabric transfer paper.

FOLLOWING A TEMPLATE

To use the quilt templates and the appliqué and embroidery patterns you'll find in this book, first enlarge them on a photocopier to the recommended percentage. For quilt templates or appliqué patterns, cut out the paper pieces and trace the shapes onto fabric with a fabric marker or pin the template (right side up) to the fabric (also right side up) to use as a guide while you cut. For embroidery patterns, transfer the design lines to your fabric for easy, follow-the-lines stitching.

BASTING

Your quilt top is cut, assembled, and embellished. Now it's finally time to start putting together that tasty quilt sandwich. Before you start sewing your layers together, you'll need to stack and baste the quilt top, batting, and backing to make sure they stay flat during the quilting process.

Iron your layers so they're smooth and free of wrinkles. Lay them out on a flat surface in the following order starting at the bottom: backing (face down), batting, and quilt top (face up). Make sure each layer is centered on top of the previous one. Starting in the center of the quilt and working out, pin, or baste, the layers together with safety or basting pins spaced about 6 inches (15.2 cm) apart (figure 10). When you've pinned your way around the quilt, check that all the layers are smooth and flat.

An important note: If you're finishing the edges using the quick turn method (where you stitch your layers together while inside out and then flip them right side out), you'll need to stack your layers in a different order before you baste them (see page 29).

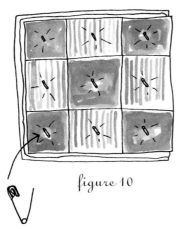

figure 10

QUILTING

Quilting is the part of the process that creates a padded, textured fabric, which is practical, decorative, and just plain fun to hold. Quilting can be done by hand or machine, but either way you should start by planning your stitch pattern. If you're doing something really complicated, you can draw out the pattern on your quilt top with chalk or a water-soluble fabric marker. The following techniques show you some of the many choices you have for making quilting patterns.

STRAIGHT-STITCH QUILTING

Straight-stitch quilting is the most basic type; it's the same type of stitch you used in piecing the quilt and other standard sewing tasks. If you're straight stitching by hand (also called a running stitch), keep your stitches short and even. For a clean finish, pull your knots through so they are hidden in the batting. On your machine, you might need to loosen the needle tension and lengthen the stitch to accommodate the thick layers. Even a mini quilt can have thick layers and some fairly large sections to keep out of the way as you sew; rolling up the edges can help you access the whole quilt as you go (figure 11).

figure 11

THE STRAIGHT TRUTH

Even a simple straight stitch has various options for giving your quilt a different look. "Stitch in the ditch" is a process that involves stitching along the seamlines of the quilt top's pieced sections, hiding your quilting stitches in the seams. You can also use the straight stitch to outline various design elements—such as appliqué or pieced shapes—to accentuate those details.

FREE-MOTION QUILTING

If you were the kind of kid who always colored with crayons outside the lines (and even if you weren't), free-motion quilting gives you complete control of the quilting stitch pattern, without any silly straight lines to worry about. For free-motion quilting on the machine, a darning foot—which has a circular opening for the needle to pass through—can help. You'll also need to disengage the automatic feed mechanism (usually called feed dogs). Control the movement of the fabric and the shape of the stitch by using two hands to spread the fabric out flat under the needle (figure 12). Guide the fabric to create any shape you like.

figure 12

TYING

Here's a technique that's quick and easy, and it can add some decorative interest to the front or back of your quilt. Tying involves connecting the quilt layers with a few stitches placed in a grid and tied. The knots can be placed on either side of the quilt. You can use embroidery floss, perle cotton, or yarn for this process (regular thread won't be thick enough). Here's how.

1 Check your batting for spacing suggestions, but 2 to 6 inches (5 to 15.2 cm) apart should be enough. You can use a ruler and chalk to mark a grid on your basted quilt top, or else place the ties randomly.

2 Thread a sharp hand-sewing needle with yarn (or whatever material you're using).

3 Stitch straight down through the quilt layers and then back up, making sure the layers don't shift as you work.

4 Tie the yarn tails in a knot. A square knot (figure 13) is easy to make and will stay firmly tied. Trim the ends to ¾ to 1 inch long (1.9 to 2.5 cm). Repeat steps 3 and 4 for each tie.

figure 13

BINDING

If a quilt top is the canvas, then binding is the picture frame. Besides adding a complementary or contrasting color to surround your mini quilt, binding is also darn useful for neatly holding the edges of your work together for years to come. The following sections give you several choices for finishing off your quilt.

MAKING YOUR OWN BINDING

You can buy premade binding at the fabric store, or you can make your own, in which case you'll have plenty of fabrics and widths to choose from. Rather than making binding pieces for each edge, it's usually easiest to make one very long length of binding and attach it around all the edges in one shot.

1 To determine the total length of the binding you'll need, add the lengths of the top, bottom, left, and right edges of the quilt, and add some extra length for safety.

2 Cut a strip following the recommended width in the pattern instructions.

3 If you need to connect strips together to make one long strip, one method is to pin and stitch the short ends together, with right sides facing, until you have one long strip, then press the seams open (figure 14).

figure 14

4 A second method for connecting strips is to pin the short ends together at a right angle, with right sides facing, and stitch diagonally across the corner (figure 15). Trim the seam allowance and press the seams open.

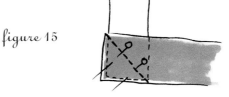

figure 15

SINGLE BINDING WITH MITERED CORNERS

Sometimes the instructions for a mini quilt will suggest a particular method, such as single-fold or double-fold binding, but it's really your call. (No one's checking up on you!) Single binding is one of the simpler methods you can use to finish a quilt.

1 After you've quilted the layers together, lay the quilt completely flat and trim the edges so the quilt top, batting, and backing are all the same size.

2 Starting midway on one edge or near a corner, pin and then stitch the right side of the batting to the right side of the fabric, folding over the starting edge (figure 16). Use the seam allowance in your instructions.

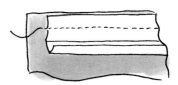

figure 16

3 Stop stitching as you approach the corner and clip the threads to remove the quilt from the machine. Fold the binding straight up over itself so a 45° angle forms at the corner (figure 17).

figure 17

4 Fold the binding straight down to make it even with the edge of the quilt and continue pinning and stitching the binding in place (figure 18). Continue working your way around the quilt, using the same process for the rest of the corners.

figure 18

5 When you near your starting point, stitch your binding strip over the folded-over starting edge of the binding strip. You don't need to fold back the raw edge at the very end of the binding strip—it'll soon be hidden.

6 Fold the binding strip over the edges (not too tightly) to the back of the quilt. Turn under the raw edge just enough to cover the seam that you just stitched. Place the prepared edge just barely over the seamline that attached the binding and pin it down along each edge. Create diagonal folds at each corner and then pin the corners in place.

7 Working from the top of the quilt, use a slipstitch by hand or stitch in the ditch to attach the binding to the back of the quilt (figure 19).

figure 19

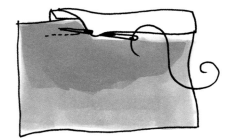

BUTTED CORNERS

Butted corners may not look as neat as mitered corners (unless you think they do), but they do give you another choice when binding.

1 Working one edge at a time (instead of a continuous strip), pin and then stitch binding along the two short edges on the right side of the quilt.

2 Fold the binding to the back, tuck under the raw edge if the binding is single-fold, and then stitch it down on the back using the slipstitch or stitching in the ditch of the seam you just created.

3 Measure and then cut the length you'll need for the long edges of the quilt, adding a little extra to each end, and attach binding to the edges as you did with the short edges.

4 Turn under the extra binding at each end and use a slipstitch to secure the ends closed (figure 20).

figure 20

DOUBLE-LAYER BINDING

This method may be a little trickier, though the steps are essentially the same as in a single-layer binding. You will end with a mini quilt with a sturdier edge. Projects with double-layer binding usually tell you how wide to cut your strips, but in general, your strips will need to be about six times wider than the final binding width you're planning.

1 Following the instructions for your project, cut the strips and then sew them together.

2 Fold the binding strip in half lengthwise with wrong sides together and then pin it to the right side of the quilt top, lining up the raw edges. Work your way around the quilt using mitered or butted corners.

3 Stitch the binding in place using the recommended seam allowance, mitering the corners (or making butted corners if you wish) as you work around the quilt (figure 21).

figure 21

4 Fold the binding to the back of the quilt and then pin and stitch it in place. Since the fabric has been folded in half, you don't have to worry about turning under any raw edges (figure 22).

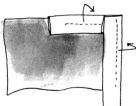

figure 22

QUICK TURNING A QUILT

Binding, schminding, you say? You want to avoid that step altogether, and not even have a border around your mini quilt? Then quick turning is the method for you. This process allows you to skip binding completely. It works particularly well if you plan on tying your quilt.

1 Stack your quilt by placing the batting on the bottom, followed by the backing, right side up, and the quilt top, centered with the right side down. Notice that this is different from the stacking described on page 24.

2 Pin the layers together along the edges, placing a few pins in the middle of the quilt to keep the layers smooth.

3 Stitch almost all the way around the outside edge of the quilt, using a ½-inch (1.3 cm) seam allowance. Leave about 10 inches (25.4 cm) unstitched for an opening to turn the quilt through.

4 Trim along the edges so all three layers are the same size, and cut across the corners to decrease bulk. Turn the quilt right side out and hand stitch the opening closed (figure 23).

figure 23

5 Baste the quilt using pins and then quilt, or tie, the layers.

HANGING A QUILT

Compared to regular quilts, mini quilts often spend a lot of their time just hanging around—up on the wall for everyone to admire. If your quilt has heavy interfacing or backing, you can add buttons or loops and a simple strand of yarn, elastic, or cord to create a hanger.

You can also consider adding a sleeve for a dowel rod or other hanging device. Cut a strip of fabric that's about 4 inches (10.2 cm) wide and almost as long as your quilt's width, turn and stitch under the short raw edges, and then pin and stitch the long edges together with right sides facing (figure 24). Turn the sleeve right side out and place it seam side down on the backing. Pin and hand stitch the sleeve in place along the top and bottom edges (figure 25). Slide a dowel rod, ribbon, or whatever you'd like through the sleeve, and you're ready to show off your newest masterpiece.

figure 24

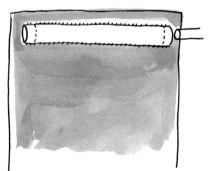

figure 25

pretty little
mini quilts projects

When it comes to quilts,
an old saying is really true:
Small is beautiful!

hearts on fire

DESIGNER

CINDY COOKSEY

$\mathcal{E}$ach of the hearts in this warm-toned quilt may differ in texture, color, and embellishment, but together they beat as one to make a beautiful design.

WHAT YOU NEED

Basic Quilting Tool Kit (page 11)

Background fabric, 18 x 16 inches (45.7 x 40.6 cm)

Low-loft batting, 18 x 16 inches (45.7 x 40.6 cm)

Cotton backing fabric, 18 x 16 inches (45.7 x 40.6 cm)

Contrasting thread for basting

16 scrap pieces of mostly red fabric for hearts, each at least 3 x 4 inches (7.6 x 10.2 cm)

Thin fusible web

Parchment paper or release paper to use with fabric fuse

Machine-quilting thread to match hearts

Perle cotton embroidery thread in a variety of weights in red, black, burgundy, and variegated

Metallic embroidery thread in silver and gold

Dark red metallic or similar fabric for binding, ¼ yard (22.9 cm)

Embellishments such as a red fabric-covered button, red beads (seed, bugle, and flat round), heart-shaped and other buttons or beads in red, metallic, or black

SEAM ALLOWANCE

None

FINISHED SIZE

14½ x 17 inches (36.8 x 43.2 cm)

WHAT YOU DO

1 Make a sandwich of the background fabric, batting, and cotton backing fabric. Pin together.

2 Baste around the outer edge. Then use a ruler and pins to locate a vertical line down the middle, and baste along the line. Use the same method to locate a horizontal line in the exact middle, and baste along that line. The basting lines will keep the silk background fabric from shifting around, and they will also help with placing the hearts.

3 Back most of the 16 3 x 4-inch (7.6 x 10.2 cm) fabric scraps with fusible web according to the manufacturer's instructions. Use release paper or parchment

SWEET HEARTS ARE MADE OF THIS

For the hearts, you can use a variety of silks, chiffon, velvet, lace, and sheers, with some solid and some printed or machine embroidered. Consider unexpected materials such as window screen and plastic "fishnet" material from a produce bag as well.

paper to protect surfaces from any melted fusible web. Some materials such as lace, window screen, and plastic fishnet will not be appropriate for fusing.

4 Trace a heart shape onto paper and cut out.

5 Pin the paper heart shape onto each fabric scrap and carefully cut out fabric hearts. There is no seam allowance.

6 Arrange the hearts on the prepared background fabric sandwich. Use the center horizontal and vertical lines to guide in placement: Place the tops of four hearts right along the horizontal line, with the bottom tips of the next row up also just touching the horizontal line. Center the hearts horizontally and place them about ½ inch (1.3 cm) apart vertically.

7 When you are happy with the arrangement, carefully iron down the hearts with fusible web on them, taking great care to keep the iron away from any window screen, plastic fishnet, or other materials that may be damaged by the heat. Pin the hearts without fusible web in place.

8 Some of the fused hearts can now be stitched down with free-motion machine quilting. Use thread that best goes with each heart—red in most cases. Stitch close to the edges, and stitch along the fabric design if desired. Leave some heart centers unquilted for later embellishment.

9 Use a hand blanket stitch around the edges of two or three of the fused hearts. Use contrasting embroidery thread such as black and metallic.

10 Use other hand embroidery to stitch down the edges of the unfused hearts, such as crisscross Xs and straight lines pointing inward.

11 Couch burgundy eyelash yarn around one heart (optional).

12 Using red perle cotton embroidery thread (red-to-burgundy hand-dyed if you can find it), hand embroider the

background fabric with random scattered stitches, about ³/₈ inch (9.5 mm) long. Make the stitches go in all directions. Continue the stitches to make a 1½-inch (3.8 cm) border on the background fabric, taking care not to extend stitches beyond this border.

13 Remove the basting thread, then trim the quilt with a rotary cutter, leaving a 1½-inch (3.8 cm) border around the hearts. This will make your quilt about 14½ inches (36.8 cm) wide and 17 inches (43.2 cm) tall.

14 Apply binding using your preferred method.

15 Embellish the centers of several hearts, but leave a few interesting ones unembellished to stand on their own. Suggestions for embellishing: Stitch a large button or charm in each upper center of several hearts. Use seed beads scattered randomly on one heart, and in snake patterns on another. Use bugle beads, round flat beads, random-sized smaller red buttons, and other distinctive-looking beads, either scattered randomly or following the design on the fabric.

16 Use extra backing fabric to create a sleeve for hanging.

around the block

This quilt is meant to have a random appearance, so be playful with your fabric selections. Try not to think too hard!

DESIGNER

REBEKA LAMBERT

WHAT YOU NEED

Basic Quilting Tool Kit (page 11)

Cotton fabric scraps in a variety of prints, each print in one of 5 colors: black, blue, green, yellow, and red

1½ yards (1.4 m) of 44-inch (1.1 m) wide white cotton for sashing and backing

2 cotton border pieces, 3 x 23 inches (7.6 x 58.4 cm)

2 cotton border pieces, 3 x 29 inches (7.6 x 73.6 cm)

Cotton batting

Pieced binding, 4 yards (3.6 m) long and 3 inches (7.6 cm) wide

SEAM ALLOWANCE

¼ inch (6 mm), unless otherwise noted

FINISHED SIZE

29 inches (73.6 cm) square

WHAT YOU DO

1 Cut nine sets of block pieces (A–E) in the following sizes.

- **A:** 2 x 3½ inches (5.1 x 8.9 cm)
- **B:** 2 x 3½ inches (5.1 x 8.9 cm)
- **C:** 1½ x 3½ inches (3.8 x 8.9 cm)
- **D:** 3 x 4½ inches (7.6 x 11.4 cm)
- **E:** 6 x 2 inches (15.2 x 5.1 cm)

Each of the five pieces within a block set should be a different color. Try to vary the colors of the pieces from set to set.

2 See the block assembly patterns on page 38. Piece each block according to one of the variations, using a ¼-inch (6 mm) seam allowance. No matter which variation, you start by sewing piece A to B along the long side. Then sew piece C to the AB. Next, sew D to ABC. Lastly, sew E to ABCD.

3 Once all the blocks are pieced, press and square them up by trimming the sides so that each block measures 6 x 6 inches (15.2 x 15.2 cm).

4 Cut the sash pieces from the white cotton in the following sizes, as shown in the sash assembly pattern on page 39.

- **aa:** 6 pieces, 2 x 6 inches (5.1 x 15.2 cm) each
- **bb:** 4 pieces, 2 x 20½ inches (5.1 x 52.1 cm) each
- **cc:** 2 pieces, 2 x 23½ inches (5.1 x 59.7 cm) each

5 Sew the sash pieces to the quilt blocks as shown in the sash assembly pattern on page 39. Begin by making three rows of blocks, with each row having three sewing blocks separated by two aa sash pieces.

6 Sew the three rows together by sewing bb sash + row 1 + bb sash + row 2 + bb sash + row 3 + bb sash. Sew the last two cc sash pieces to either side of the quilt top.

7 Sew the 23-inch (58.4 cm) border strips to the top and the bottom of the quilt top. Sew the 29-inch (73.6 cm) border strips to either side of the quilt top. Trim the border pieces as need to square up the top. Iron the quilt top.

8 Cut the quilt backing and batting a few inches larger than the finished quilt top. Make the quilt sandwich by layering the backing (right side down), the batting, then the quilt top (right side up). Baste the quilt together with safety pins or basting pins.

9 Quilt as desired, then trim the excess backing and batting.

10 Make your binding by sewing various 3-inch (7.6 cm) wide scraps together. After sewing the pieces end to end, fold the binding in half right sides together, then press.

11 Starting at the middle of one side of the quilt and using a ½-inch (1.3 cm) seam allowance, sew the binding to the right side of the quilt with the raw edges of the binding lined up with the raw edge of the quilt.

BLOCK ASSEMBLY PATTERNS

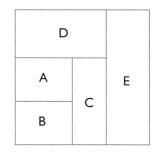

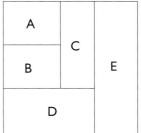

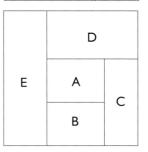

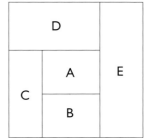

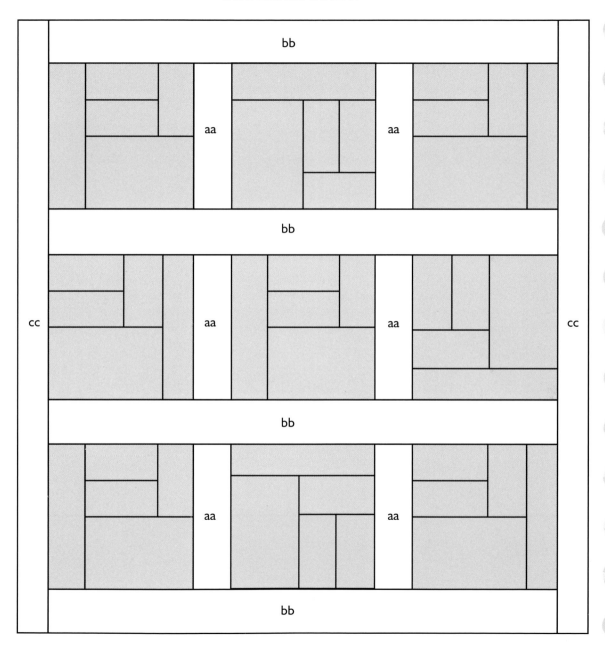

days of summer

There's nothing better than a good book on a sunny, school-free day, and this little quilt perfectly captures that sweet childhood moment.

DESIGNER

SHELECE JORGENSEN

WHAT YOU NEED

Basic Quilting Tool Kit (page 11)

Cream fabric, 9 x 5½ inches
(22.9 x 14 cm)

Green cotton, 9 x 2½ inches
(22.9 x 6.4 cm)

Brown cotton for backing, 12 x 9
inches (30.5 x 22.9 cm)

Brown, white, and yellow thread

Solid yellow fabric, 2½ x 2½
inches (6.4 x 6.4 cm)

Brown fabric, 2½ x 2 inches
(6.4 x 5.1 cm)

White fabric, 2 x 1 inches
(5.1 x 2.5 cm)

Skin-tone fabric, 2 x 2 inches
(5.1 x 5.1 cm)

Orange pattern cotton,
3½ x 2 inches (8.9 x 5.1 cm)

Sheet of card stock (optional)

Black, brown, and red embroidery
floss

SEAM ALLOWANCE

¼ inch (6 mm), unless otherwise
noted

FINISHED SIZE

9 x 7 inches (22.9 x 17.8 cm)

WHAT YOU DO

1 Hand-sew the cream and green pieces together to make the sky-and-grass background for the appliqué.

2 Lay the cream-and-green quilt front on the brown backing piece. Fold the quilt backing edges toward the front (first the top and bottom and then the sides) to make a self-binding. Stitch down the edges with brown sewing thread. Iron flat.

3 Cut out the small fabric pieces to the shapes you wish for the sun, book, face, and dress, using the photo as inspiration.

4 Arrange the fabric pieces on the quilt top and pin in place. Begin appliquéing, starting with the book page, then the book. Next appliqué the dress, and lastly appliqué the face and the sun.

5 Use embroidery floss to add little knots for the eyes, up and down stitches for a book title, and straight stitches (tacked down at the elbows and knees) for the arms and legs. The hair is made of brown embroidery floss sewn in a simple satin stitch, and the red hair ties are small stitches wrapping around the ponytails.

ADDING ANOTHER DIMENSION

To give some depth to the face and the sun shapes you make in step 3, cut circle shapes from white card stock paper in the final size and shape you want each to be. Cut each fabric ¼ inch (6 mm) larger than its circle, run a few loose stitches around the edge of the fabric, place the card stock inside the ring of stitches, and cinch the fabric tight around the paper, securing it with a knot.

6 Add some decorative quilting stitches around the sun and in the grass area.

7 If you wish, use black embroidery floss to add your "signature" in the upper left corner as the designer did here. Iron the quilt flat, and it's ready to hang or frame.

center of attention

Capture the glory of autumn year-round with this beautiful and simple design.

DESIGNER

RUTH SINGER

WHAT YOU NEED

Basic Quilting Tool Kit (page 11)

Leaf templates

Circles (such as embroidery hoops) to draw circles around

Cream cotton, 32-inch (81.3 cm) square

Pink cotton, 32-inch (81.3 cm) square

Cotton batting, 32 inches (81.3 cm)

18 scraps of prewashed fabric in different materials and textures, about 4 inches (10.2 cm) square each

¼ yard (22.9 cm) lightweight iron-on interfacing

Coordinating fabric scraps to make about 4 yards (3.6 m) of binding strips

Variegated embroidery thread for quilting

SEAM ALLOWANCE

None

FINISHED SIZE

18¼ inches (46.4 cm) square

WHAT YOU DO

1 To prepare the 18 leaves, first iron interfacing onto the back of the fabric scraps. Trace a different leaf design onto each scrap and cut out.

2 Arrange 17 leaves in a circular design about 16 inches (40.6 cm) in diameter on the cream fabric and pin. Put the last leaf in the center. Hand stitch the leaves into place using a matching sewing thread, or a contrasting embroidery thread if you prefer.

3 Draw the quilting lines shown in the photo with a fabric marker, using embroidery hoops or plates to create the circles. The center circles are 4 inches (10.2 cm), 9 inches (22.9 cm), and 13 inches (33 cm) in diameter. The corner circles are 5 inches (12.7 cm) and 3 inches (7.6 cm) in diameter.

4 Layer the quilt with the pink backing face down, then the batting, then the quilt top facing up. Use safety pins or baste in place.

5 Hand quilt the circles through all layers in large running stitches, using the embroidery thread. Start at the innermost center circle and work out. You can start and fasten the thread between the backing and the batting.

6 Remove the pins or basting and trim the quilt down to 28 inches (71.1 cm) square, cutting close to the corner stitching.

7 To make the binding, cut strips 2½ inches (6.4 cm) wide in a range of different fabrics to match or coordinate with the leaves. Join together to make a total length of about 4 yards (3.6 m).

8 Bind the quilt by your preferred method.

TREE HUGGING

It only makes sense in a quilt design that celebrates the diversity of nature: Organic cotton was used here in the quilt top, the backing, and the batting.

checkered past

You'll have plenty of squares to play with in this elegant geometric quilt.

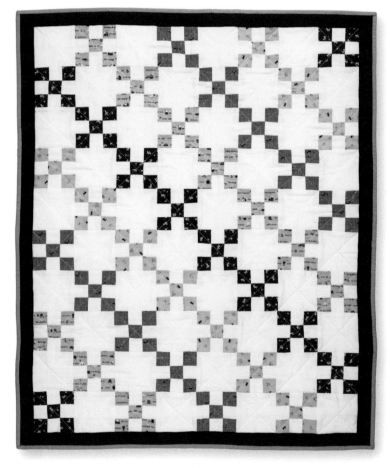

DESIGNER

DORIE BLAISDELL SCHWARZ

WHAT YOU NEED

Basic Quilting Tool Kit (page 11)

Note: All fabric is 44 inches (1.1 m) wide.

¼ yard (22.9 cm) each of two red print cottons

¼ yard (22.9 cm) each of two gold print cottons

½ yard (45.7 cm) white cotton

¼ yard (22.9 cm) red cotton for the border

1 yard (.9 m) white cotton for backing

Low-loft cotton batting

¼ yard (22.9 cm) gold cotton for binding

SEAM ALLOWANCE

¼ inch (6 mm)

FINISHED SIZE

26½ x 32½ inches (67.3 x 82.5 cm)

WHAT YOU DO

1 From each of the two red and two gold fabric prints, cut five 1½-inch (3.8 cm) wide strips, each at least 15 to 16 inches (38.1 to 40.6 cm) long. Cut a total of 16 white strips of the same size. Also, cut 40 3½-inch (8.9 cm) squares from the white fabric.

2 For each of the red and gold prints, do the following. Sew three strips together in this pattern: color, white, color. Repeat the pattern with three more strips. Then sew three strips together as white, color, white. You'll have three strips of three, using a total of five color strips and four white strips. Press the seams toward the colored fabric. Cut each strip of three into 1½-inch (3.8 cm) segments.

3 Arrange three segments in a checkerboard pattern (figure 1). Stitch the segments together. Repeat this step until you have 10 checkerboard squares for each of the four colors.

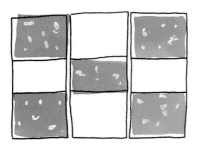

figure 1

4 Lay out the quilt as shown in the photo, alternating checkerboard squares with plain white squares.

5 Sew the top together: Make strips by sewing together all the squares in each horizontal row. Then sew the rows together, making sure to line up the seams between blocks.

6 Cut two 1½ x 24½-inch (3.8 x 62.2 cm) strips and two 1½ x 32½-inch (3.8 x 82.5 cm) strips from the solid red fabric. Add the border by first sewing the two shorter red strips to the shorter ends of the quilt, then sewing the remaining strips to the longer sides.

7 Make the quilt sandwich: Lay out the backing on a flat surface and smooth out any wrinkles. Lay the cotton batting on top, then cover with the quilt top. Smooth all the layers, and then baste them using safety pins.

8 Quilt the quilt using diagonal lines that run through all the large white squares and diago-nal lines that run through all the checked squares. When you're done, each 3-inch (7.6 cm) unit will have an X through it.

9 Bind the quilt using the solid gold fabric and a ¼-inch (6 mm) binding (see pages 26–28 on binding techniques).

drop everything

*T*he teardrop shapes on this little quilt give you a chance to showcase seven of the most varied scraps in your stash.

DESIGNER

CANDACE TODD

WHAT YOU NEED

Basic Quilting Tool Kit (page 11)

Fusible web

7 scraps of cotton patterned fabrics in stripes, polka dots, eyelet, etc., each 4 x 3 inches (10.2 x 7.6 cm)

1 piece linen fabric, 15 x 12 inches (38.1 x 30.5 cm)

1 piece cotton polka-dot fabric, 15 x 12 inches (38.1 x 30.5 cm)

1 piece cotton batting, 15 x 12 inches (38.1 x 30.5 cm)

¼ yard (22.9 cm) red cotton fabric for binding

SEAM ALLOWANCE

None

FINISHED SIZE

15½ x 12 inches (39.4 x 30.5 cm)

WHAT YOU DO

1 Iron fusible web onto the backs of all seven fabric scraps. Draw and cut out a teardrop template about 2½ inches (6.4 cm) long and 1½ inches (3.8 cm) wide, then trace a teardrop onto the back of each fabric scrap. Cut out the teardrops and remove the paper backing.

2 Place the teardrop pieces in alternating directions on the linen fabric, as shown in the photo. Press with the iron to adhere.

3 Place the backing fabric face down, then the batting, and then the linen piece facing up. Pin together. Place pins throughout the quilt about every 2 inches (5.1 cm).

4 Using your sewing machine, stitch around each teardrop, reversing a little at the beginning and the end to anchor your stitches. Cut off any threads.

5 Draw stitching lines onto the quilt with a fabric pen. Lower the feed dogs on your sewing machine and stitch through all three layers of the quilt on the stitching line marks. Remove the pins when necessary. Trim all threads.

6 Attach binding using the double-fold method. Cut the binding fabric into 2½-inch (6.4 cm) strips and sew the length together until you have enough to go around your quilt plus a little extra. Iron the strip in half lengthwise. Pin raw edges of the binding to the quilt top's edge and start sewing along the raw edge. Do not start your sewing at the corner.

7 When you come to a corner, stop about ¼ inch (6 mm) from the edge. Fold the strip straight up, making a diagonal line. Then fold the strip straight back down over the fold you just made and resume stitching ¼ inch (6 mm) from the edge.

8 Wrap the folded edge of the binding over the quilt edge and onto the back. Hand-sew the binding to the back of the quilt using the invisible hem stitch.

corner store

WHAT YOU NEED

Basic Quilting Tool Kit (page 11)

Note: All fabric is 44 inches
(1.1 m) wide.

1 yard (.9 m) cotton background
fabric in red or color of your
choice

Triangle corners from scraps
(1930s reproduction fabrics or
scraps on hand)

1 yard (.9 m) backing fabric

2 yards (1.8 m) rickrack to match
background fabric

Perle cotton quilting thread

Hand-quilting needle

SEAM ALLOWANCE

¼ inch (6 mm)

FINISHED SIZE

17½ x 22 inches (44.5 x 55.9 cm)

DESIGNER

LYNN HARRIS

This little quilt is a livelier version of the
traditional Exquisite quilt block. Try making it with
all solids, or mix things up by using a print for the
background and solids for the triangles.

WHAT YOU DO

1 Cut 63 3-inch (7.6 cm) squares of background fabric.

2 Sew scraps of fabric onto the diagonal corners of each background square (figure 1) so that when pressed open the scrap fabric will cover that corner of the background square (figure 2). Press open.

figure 1   figure 2

3 Trim the corner of each background square to a ¼-inch (6 mm) seam allowance behind the corner fabric. Then trim the squares to 3 inches (7.6 cm).

4 Lay out the squares in nine rows of seven, with all squares oriented in the same direction, and sew together. Press.

5 Sew the rickrack to the right side of the quilt top, with the edges of the rickrack even with the edge of the quilt.

6 Press and measure the quilt top, and cut a piece of backing fabric to the same size. Place the quilt top on the backing fabric right sides together and pin around the edge.

7 Sew around the quilt just inside the previous (rickrack) stitching so that the first stitching will not show when turned. Leave a gap on one edge to turn.

8 Turn the quilt right side out and press. Gently pull on the rickrack points as you press the edge. Slipstitch the gap closed.

9 Baste the layers together. Hand-quilt with perle cotton thread. To avoid quilting over so many seams, quilt only in the background fabrics.

SET YOURSELF FREE

The technique used for sewing these squares, called "liberated piecing," was introduced by Gwen Marston, a quilting teacher and author. Odd-shaped scraps will produce more variety, so play around with the design by varying the size and shape of the triangles.

autumn breeze

DESIGNER

LOUISE PAPAS

After composing this seasonal scene, you may be inspired to gather fabrics in different tones to complete a series of quilts. Spring Mist or Summer Wind, anyone?

WHAT YOU NEED

Basic Quilting Tool Kit (page 11)

22 inches (55.9 cm) cream cotton, such as quilter's muslin or homespun

10 inches (25.4 cm) autumnal floral print cotton

Fat sixteenth (22.9 x 27.9 cm) of light brown patterned cotton

Fat sixteenth (22.9 x 27.9 cm) each of small-print yellow, red, brown, and orange cotton

Cream thread

23½ inches (59.7 cm) cotton in a coordinating color for backing

23½ inches (59.7 cm) cotton batting

Perle embroidery thread in cream

6 inches (15.2 cm) orange-and-cream-striped cotton fabric for binding

SEAM ALLOWANCE

¼ inch (6 mm)

FINISHED SIZE

19 x 20 inches (48.3 x 50.8 cm)

WHAT YOU DO

1 To make the quilt top, cut the cream fabric to 21 x 20 inches (53.3 x 50.8 cm). It will be cut to size before the binding goes on so that the edges are neat.

2 Draw a set of tree top, tree trunk, and leaf patterns onto tracing paper and cut these out for templates.

3 Pin the tree top and tree trunk templates onto the appropriate floral and light-brown fabrics and cut one of each. Take the leaf template and cut 26 leaves from a mixture of the red, orange, yellow, and brown fabrics.

4 Using the photo as a guide, place the tree trunk in position on the quilt top and pin. Appliqué the tree trunk onto the quilt top using the cream thread. Repeat with the tree top.

5 Using the photo as a guide, place the leaves on the quilt and pin them into position. Appliqué them onto the quilt top.

6 Cut the backing fabric and batting 1 inch (2.5 cm) larger than the quilt top. Place the backing right side down and place the batting on top. Then place the quilt top onto the batting right side up. Smooth it down so there are no wrinkles, and pin through all the layers with safety pins.

7 Using the perle thread, quilt ⅛ inch (3 mm) away from the edge of the tree top, tree trunk, and leaves.

8 Using a washable marker or pencil, mark up the branch and trunk details and wind swirls. Quilt these lines using the perle thread.

9 Trim the quilt to measure 19 inches (48.3 cm) wide and 20 inches (50.8 cm) high.

10 Bind the quilt with your preferred method, using the orange-and-cream fabric.

blue pools

*T*his combination of geometric shapes and free-form
stitching is a snap to make. Dive right in!

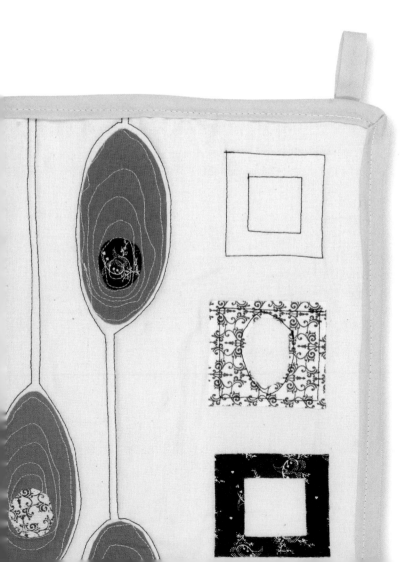

WHAT YOU NEED

Basic Quilting Tool Kit (page 11)

⅓ yard (30.5 cm) each of cream and
aqua cotton

¼ yard (22.9 cm) polyester batting

¼ yard (22.9 cm) periwinkle cotton

Fusible web

Scraps of light blue and dark blue
print fabrics

Cream and navy thread

Light blue double-fold bias tape

SEAM ALLOWANCE

None

FINISHED SIZE

10½ x 18½ inches (26.7 x 47 cm)

DESIGNER

AMANDA CARESTIO

WHAT YOU DO

1 Cut the cream fabric to 10½ x 18½ inches (26.7 x 47 cm) and the batting and aqua fabric to 11 x 19 inches (27.9 x 48.3 cm).

2 Fuse a 4½ x 13-inch (11.4 x 33 cm) section of fusible web to the wrong side of the periwinkle fabric. Using a template you create or cutting freehand, cut six ovals that measure about 2 x 4 inches (5.1 x 10.2 cm).

3 Iron the ovals in place on top of the cream fabric, staggering the shapes to create three rows.

4 Fuse a 6 x 6-inch (15.2 x 15.2 cm) square of fusible web to the back of the light blue and dark blue print fabrics. From the light blue print, cut two 1-inch (2.5 cm) diameter circles and one 2½ x 2-inch (6.4 x 5.1 cm) rectangle. From the dark blue print, cut four circles and one rectangle using the same dimensions.

5 Cut an oval from the center of the light blue rectangle and a square from the inside of the dark blue rectangle.

6 Fuse the circles in place on top of the ovals. Baste the quilt top to the batting with pins, and free-motion stitch the shapes in place using cream thread. Start in the center of the circle and work your way out in oblong spirals. Once you have the ovals stitched down, you can unpin the layers.

7 Baste the top, batting, and backing together with pins and switch to blue thread. Using the photo as a guide, stitch up to and around each oval shape, working up the left side and down the right side of each row.

8 Working from the top right down, create a stitched 2-inch (5.1 cm) square (with a smaller square inside), fuse and then stitch the light blue print rectangle in place, and fuse and stitch the dark blue print rectangle in place. Create a row of four 5½-inch (14 cm) tall stitched rectangles of varying widths below the three rectangles.

9 Sandwich the quilt layers between the fold of the bias tape and topstitch the tape in place, going through all the layers at the same time. Cut two 3-inch (7.6 cm) lengths of bias tape, fold them both in half, and attach them along the top edge of the quilt to create hanging tabs.

A THINNER SANDWICH

It's a little easier to free-motion stitch the ovals in place through only the quilt top and the batting, but you could perform this step after all three layers (including the backing) are basted together. Doing it that way would display more stitching on the back of the quilt.

square deal

ℬlocks of bold color, squiggly lines, and delicate
French knots show that sometimes the simplest ideas are the best.

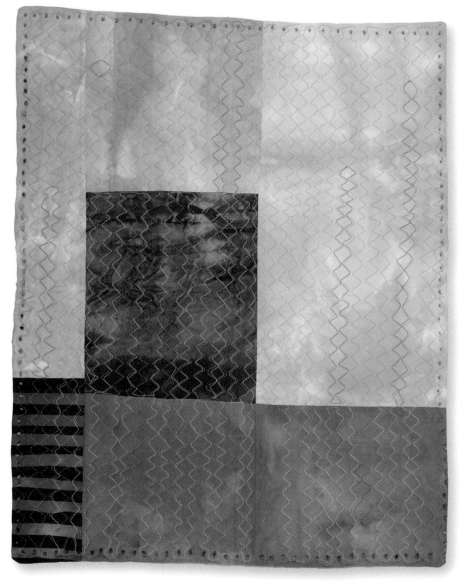

MALKA DUBRAWSKY

WHAT YOU NEED

Basic Quilting Tool Kit (page 11)

Template (page 141)

Note: All fabric is 44 inches (1.1 m) wide.

¼ yard (22.9 cm) raspberry cotton (piece 1)

¼ yard (22.9 cm) chartreuse cotton (pieces 2, 5, and 6)

¼ yard (22.9 cm) kelly green cotton (pieces 3 and 4)

⅛ yard (11.4 cm) raspberry-and-orange-striped cotton (piece 7)

Embroidery hoop

Turquoise embroidery thread

Embroidery needle

½ yard (45.7 cm) cotton batting

½ yard (45.7 cm) teal cotton for backing

Chartreuse thread

Machine-quilting thread in orange, turquoise, and white

SEAM ALLOWANCE

¼ inch (6 mm)

FINISHED SIZE

18 x 23 inches (45.7 x 58.4 cm)

WHAT YOU DO

1 Use a copier to enlarge the quilt template on page 141. Cut apart the seven pieces.

2 Pin piece 1 to the raspberry fabric and cut along the edges adding the ¼ inch (6 mm) seam allowance. Repeat with the other six template pieces, pinning them to their matching fabrics and cutting.

3 Sew pieces 1 and 2 together along their short edges. Press the seam to one side. It's best to alternate sides where seams intersect.

4 Following the template diagram, sew piece 3 to the strip containing pieces 1 and 2 along its long edge. Press to one side. Then sew pieces 4 and 5 together along their short edges. Press to one side.

5 Sew the strip containing pieces 4 and 5 to the strip containing pieces 1, 2, and 3 along the long edge. Press to one side.

6 Sew pieces 6 and 7 together along their short edges. Press to one side. Then sew the strip containing pieces 6 and 7 to the rest of the quilt top along the long edge.

7 With a ruler and pencil, mark the perimeter of the quilt top to place French knots, with knots about ½ inch (1.3 cm) from each edge and spaced ½ inch (1.3 cm) apart.

8 Place the quilt top in the embroidery hoop and, using turquoise embroidery thread, stitch French knots where marked. Reposition the embroidery hoop as needed.

9 Lay the batting on your cutting mat, and lay the teal backing fabric right side up on the batting. Lay the quilt top right side down on the backing and batting. Pin the layers together and trim them even.

10 Sew the layers together, leaving a 9-inch (22.9 cm) gap along one side. Trim the corners. Turn the quilt right side out, making sure to poke out the corners.

11 Press the quilt flat and turn under a ¼-inch (6 mm) seam allowance at the gap. Pin. Using chartreuse thread and a hand-sewing needle, slip-stitch the gap closed.

12 Lay the quilt on the cutting mat and baste with safety pins about every 4 inches (10.2 cm). Free-motion machine-quilt with an allover squiggle pattern in orange thread, removing pins as you go. Accent some of the squiggles by machine-quilting in white and turquoise.

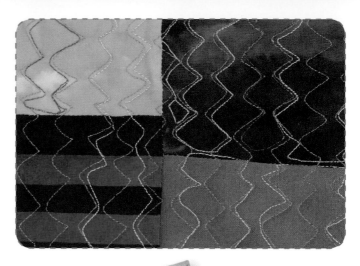

COMBINATION PLATE

Can't find a striped fabric you like for the corner of the quilt? You can make your own striped fabric by seaming together strips of 1-inch (2.5 cm) wide fabric in shades of raspberry and orange (or the colors of your choice).

bright teeth

Two endless rows of triangles circle around delicate embroidery in this classic quilt.

WHAT YOU NEED

Basic Quilting Tool Kit (page 11)

¾ yard (68.6 cm) white cotton

Assorted fabrics in bright colors, enough for 28 squares, each 2⅜ inches (6.1 cm)

Green embroidery floss

Thin cotton batting, 23 x 18 inches (58.4 x 45.7 cm)

¼ yard (22.9 inches) green cotton for binding

SEAM ALLOWANCE

None

FINISHED SIZE

15 x 21 inches (38.1 x 53.3 cm)

DESIGNER

DORIE BLAISDELL SCHWARZ

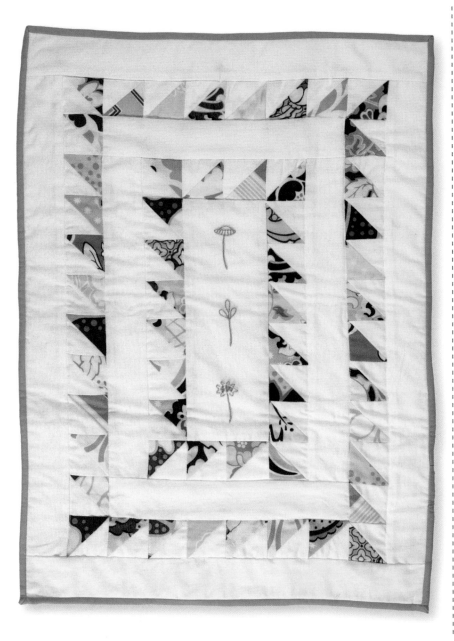

WHAT YOU DO

1 From the white cotton, cut the following pieces:

- One 23 x 18 inches (58.4 x 45.7 cm)

- 28 2⅜-inch (6.1 cm) squares

- One 9½ x 3½ inches (24.1 x 8.9 cm)

- Two 12½ x 2 inches (31.8 x 5.1 cm)

- Two 9½ x 2 inches (24.1 x 5.1 cm)

- Two 18½ x 2 inches (47 x 5.1 cm)

- Two 15½ x 2 inches (39.4 x 5.1 cm)

2 From the brightly colored fabrics, cut 28 2⅜-inch (6.1 cm) squares.

3 On the wrong side of each colored 2⅜-inch (6.1 cm) square, mark a line using a straight edge and pencil that goes diagonally across the square, from one point to its opposite point.

4 Bring together one white square and one colored square and line them up, right sides facing. Sew them together by sewing ¼ inch (6 mm) on each side of the diagonally drawn line. Repeat with the rest of the squares.

5 Cut the squares on the pencil line. Each sewn square becomes two half-square triangle units. Press the triangles open into squares, pressing the seams toward the colored fabric.

6 You now have all the pieces for the quilt top. Lay them all out so that they match the layout of the quilt in the photo. Pay careful attention to the direction of the triangle slant on each corner.

7 Starting with the rows around the center, sew the half-square triangles to each other, forming strips. You'll have two strips of six half-square triangle units, two strips of four half-square triangle units, two strips of ten half-square triangle units, and two strips of eight half-square triangle units.

8 Sew the six unit strips to the long sides of the 9½ x 3½-inch (24.1 x 8.9 cm) rectangle. Sew the four unit strips to the short side. Continue to build out from the center in this way. Next sew the 12½ x 2-inch (31.8 x 5.1 cm) white rectangles to the long side of the center, then add the 9½ x 2-inch (24.1 x 5.1 cm) white rectangles, and so on, until you have finished the top.

9 Embroider the motifs in the center using two strands of the green floss. The quilt shown here includes plant motifs with stem stitch for the stems, lazy daisy stitch for the lowest flower's petals, French knots for its center, and backstitch for the rest.

10 Make the quilt sandwich with white cotton on bottom, cotton batting in the middle, and the quilt top on top. Use safety pins to baste through all the layers

11 Quilt the quilt by "stitching in the ditch"—stitch along all the seam lines of all the rectangles. Start in the middle and work your way out.

12 Bind the quilt using ¼-inch (6 mm) binding.

yard tale

Want to uproot the felt radishes and plant broccoli instead?
Removable felt pieces make it easy to change this quilt to suit your taste.

DESIGNER

ROXANNE BEAUVAIS

WHAT YOU NEED

Basic Quilting Tool Kit (page 11)

Templates (page 139–140)

Wool felt, 18 x 12-inch (45.7 x 30.5 cm) sheets, one light blue and one tan

Purple and tan thread

⅓ yard (30.5 cm) wood-grain fabric

Low-loft cotton batting, 20 x 17½ inches (50.8 x 44.5 cm)

Cotton backing fabric, 20 x 17½ inches (50.8 x 44.5 cm)

Wool felt, 9 x 12-inch (22.9 x 30.5 cm) sheets, in purple, blue green, dark blue, brown, gray, olive green, and yellow

Embroidery floss in yellow, gray, brown, blue green, olive green, red, orange, and white

Embroidery needle

Clear craft glue

SEAM ALLOWANCE

¼ inch (6 mm)

FINISHED SIZE

19¾ x 17¼ inches (50.2 x 43.8 cm)

WHAT YOU DO

1 Cut the light blue wool felt to 17¼ x 7¾ inches (43.8 x 19.7 cm). Cut the tan wool felt to 17¼ x 7¼ inches (43.8 x 18.4 cm). Sew the long ends of these two pieces together on a sewing machine with tan thread. Press the seam flat. This creates the sky and ground portions of the quilt top.

2 Cut four strips of the wood-grain fabric for the border in the following sizes:

• Two pieces, 19 x 2 inches (48.3 x 5.1 cm)

• Two pieces, 21¾ x 2 inches (55.2 x 5.1 cm)

3 Place the 19-inch (48.3 cm) strip of wood-grain fabric on the short, left side of the quilt top with right sides together. Center the strip, leaving a 1-inch (2.5 cm) overhang on either end. Starting ¼ inch (6 mm) in from the corner of the quilt, sew the wood-grain strip to the felt. Stop ¼ inch (6 mm) from the edge of the quilt. Following the same instructions, attach the other three strips to the corresponding edges of the quilt.

figure 1

4 Press all seams open. Turn the quilt over, create 45-degree angles at each corner, and press (figure 1). Unfold, match the pressed lines, and pin and sew. Be sure not to sew into the felt. Trim the excess and continue in this manner for the remaining corners. Press.

5 Sandwich the quilt layers— quilt top, batting, backing fabric. Carefully smooth out all layers and pin together using safety pins. As you add items and embroider the quilt, the pins may be removed.

6 Cut out felt pieces using the templates on page 139–140, or create your own clothing and vegetables in appropriate sizes. For the quilt shown here, you'll need a roof, door, treetop, tree trunk, garden plot, shirt, pants, and two each of carrots, onions, and radishes.

7 Cut a 6⅞-inch (17.4 cm) square from the blue-green felt for the house. Cut squares from the yellow wool felt for the windows in the following dimensions:

• Two 1⅛-inch (2.8 cm) squares

• One 1½ x 2-inch (3.8 x 5.1 cm) square

8 Cut a strip of dark blue felt ⅝ x 6⅞ inches (1.6 x 17.4 cm). Center the strip halfway down the felt house and sew it onto the house with purple thread. Place the purple roof piece on top of the house with a ¼-inch (6 mm) overlap and topstitch the roof and house together using purple thread on a sewing machine.

9 Apply the windows to the house using yellow embroidery floss and a running stitch by hand. Use a running stitch and gray embroidery floss to apply the door. Use the same floss to place a French knot on the door for a knob. Using a backstitch and brown embroidery floss, create the scalloped roof pattern, as shown on the template.

10 Apply the house to the quilt using a running stitch. Use gray embroidery floss on the house section and brown embroidery floss on the roof section.

11 Attach the garden pocket using brown embroidery floss and a running stitch. Start stitching on the short, right side, continuing across the bottom, up the left side and just around the curve. Leave the top flap open. Create rows in your garden by measuring 2 inches (5.1 cm) from either side of the pocket opening and stitching down the pocket to create three smaller sections.

12 Pin the green treetop to the quilt. Apply the tree trunk over it and stitch it down using brown embroidery floss and a running stitch. Apply a running stitch around the treetop with olive green embroidery floss.

16 To make the binding, cut 80 inches (2 m) worth of 2½-inch (6.4 cm) wide strips of the wood-grain fabric. Attach the strips at an angle to create one long continuous strip. Fold the piece in half (right sides facing out) and press.

17 Starting several inches from a corner, lay the binding along the edge of the quilt with the raw edges matching up. Pin and sew. At the corners, stop ¼ inch (6 mm) from the edge. Fold the binding at an angle and start the next side ¼ inch (6 mm) in. Continue this all the way around, stopping several inches from your starting point. Connect your binding pieces, trim the excess, and then continue sewing the binding to the quilt.

18 Press the binding back. Pin in place and hand-stitch the binding to the back of the quilt.

13 Cut nine small round pieces for rocks from the gray felt. Using gray embroidery floss, stitch down the rocks to create a path from the front door to the garden. Each rock requires just a few stitches to hold it securely in place.

14 Stitch details on the clothes using various strands of embroidery floss. Apply a very small amount of clear craft glue to the knots on the back of each piece to secure them. Stitch details on the vegetables using a running stitch for the stems and a satin stitch for the vegetables. Use all strands of green, orange, red, and white floss accordingly. Again, apply a small amount of clear craft glue to secure the knots.

15 Apply the clothesline by making a French knot with the tan thread next to the house. Bring the thread back up and stretch it across the quilt to meet the tree. Leave a bit of sag in the thread. Bring the thread down and back up and make a French knot at the tree.

CHANGE OF SEASONS

The photo above shows the house and garden without decoration. Make a variety of felt pieces to use when there's frost on the pumpkin or spring flowers are blooming.

ring of roses mandala

DESIGNER

CHEYENNE GOH

$\mathcal{Q}$uilts have to be flat and square? Not if you don't want them to be, as proved by this dynamic creation.

WHAT YOU NEED

Basic Quilting Tool Kit (page 11)

Chocolate brown jute (gunny/burlap), 44 x 22 inches (111.8 x 55.9 cm)

Taupe linen, 18 inches (45.7 cm) square

Light brown cotton, 14 inches (35.6 cm) square

Gray fabric scrap, 19¾ x 2¾ inches (50.2 x 7 cm)

Black fabric scrap, one piece 8 x 2¾ inches (20.3 x 7 cm) and one 5½ x 2¾ inches (14 x 7 cm)

45 black/gray suiting scraps, 2¾ x 19¾ inches (7 x 50.2 cm) each

7 purple fabric scraps, 2¾ x 23½ inches (7 x 59.7 cm) each

4 magenta fabric scraps, 2¾ x 23½ inches (7 x 59.7 cm) each

4 red fabric scraps, 2¾ x 23½inches (7 x 59.7 cm) each

6 peach fabric scraps, 2¾ x 23½ inches (7 x 59.7 cm) each

6 pink fabric scraps, 2¾ x 23½ inches (7 x 59.7 cm) each

12 green fabric scraps, 2¾ x 23½ inches (7 x 59.7 cm) each

6 blue fabric scraps, 2¾ x 23½ inches (7 x 59.7 cm) each

Thimble

Pliers

2 gray fabric scraps for flaps, 2¾ x 6 inches (7 x 15.2 cm) each

2 yards (1.8 m) black piping

SEAM ALLOWANCE

None

FINISHED SIZE

20 inches (50.8 cm) in diameter

WHAT YOU DO

MAKING THE ROUND BASE

1 Cut the jute fabric into two circles with a diameter of 19½ inches (49.5 cm). Set one aside as the backing. Cut the linen into a circle with a diameter of 16 inches (40.6 cm). Cut the light brown cotton into a circle with a diameter of 12 inches (30.5 cm).

2 Fold the jute circle in half, then into quarters to find its center. Mark it with a pin. Do the same with the linen and cotton circles.

3 Align the center of the linen circle with the center of the jute circle and pin the linen circle into place. Make a ⅜-inch (9.5 mm) fold on the raw edge of the linen circle and machine-sew along its circumference with the fold between the linen and the jute. Do the same with the cotton circle on the linen circle.

4 To make the thin strip between the jute and the linen, join the short sides of the two black and one 19¾-inch (50.2 cm) gray fabric scraps with the black between the gray, using a flat seam. Fold the joined piece in half, lengthwise, and iron in the crease. Fold the edges toward the center. Pin both sides together, then machine-sew along the edge.

5 Pin the finished strip to a point where the jute meets the linen. Continue pinning the strip along the circumference of the linen circle. Machine-sew both edges of the strip.

MAKING A RECYCLED ROSE

6 For each rose, join together the 2¾-inch (7 cm) edges of a black suiting fabric scrap and a colored 23½-inch (7 x 59.7 cm) long scrap with a flat seam. Fold the joined piece in half, lengthwise, and iron in the crease. Fold the long edges toward the center. Pin both sides (figure 1), then machine-sew along the long edge.

figure 1

7 Make a ⅜-inch (9.5 mm) fold on the unfinished tips and machine-sew flat. Wind the finished colored tip around itself and continue winding until the end of the strip. Push a pin through the body of the rose to hold it in shape.

8 Blind stitch the other finished tip onto the body of the rose. To ensure the wound fabric doesn't slip, put a stitch from one side of the rose through all the layers, coming out the other side. Because the layers can be thick, go through the fabric layers a section at a time, using the thimble to push the needle and the pliers to pull the needle through (figure 2).

figure 2

MAKING THE ROSE MANDALA

9 Alternately arrange the four red and four magenta roses into a line. Simple stitch each to its neighbor with five stitches. End the last stitch on the wrong side of the group and make a knot.

10 Using a purple rose as the center, ring it with the line of red and magenta roses. Using the same simple five stitches as above, attach each rose to the purple center.

11 Alternately arrange the six peach and six pink roses into a line. Attach each to its neighbor and then attach the first of this line to a rose in the red/magenta group.

12 Work your way down the line until the end. To complete the ring, attach the last rose to the first of the line.

13 Attach the remaining six purple roses to each peach rose. Group two green roses with a blue rose. Attach them together in a triangular shape. Place each trio between the purple roses, with the green roses next to the ring of peach/pink roses.

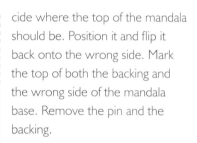

ASSEMBLING THE QUILT

14 Center the rose mandala on the round base. Flip it so that the base is on top of the mandala. Hand stitch each purple and blue rose onto the round base, using five stitches and ending with a secure knot.

15 To attach the backing and hanging flaps, first fold one gray hanging flap lengthwise. Press the crease. Fold the edges in toward the center and pin the two sides together. Machine-sew the edges together. Repeat with the other hanging flap.

16 Tuck in the tips to neaten them and fold the flap to half its height. Pin the two sides together. Repeat with the other flap.

17 With the wrong side of the rose mandala facing up, place the backing jute circle on top of it. Pin them together to align them.

18 Flip the whole thing back to the right side to de-cide where the top of the mandala should be. Position it and flip it back onto the wrong side. Mark the top of both the backing and the wrong side of the mandala base. Remove the pin and the backing.

19 Place the hanging flaps on the backing, ⅜ inch (9.5 mm) from the top edge of the circle. Pin them 9¾ inches (24.8 cm) apart. Machine-sew a ¾-inch (1.9 cm) tall rectangle onto the tips of the flaps to attach them onto the backing.

20 Hand stitch both sides of the loop of the hanging flaps to the backing.

21 Fold in ⅜ inch (9.5 mm) from the edge of both the backing and the mandala base. Pin down along the circumference. Tack the edges together.

22 Pin the black piping around the edge of the circles, enclosing the edges. Machine-sew the piping all along the circumference.

kelp wanted

WHAT YOU NEED

Basic Quilting Tool Kit (page 11)

⅓ yard (30.5 cm) cream cotton

⅓ yard (30.5 cm) polyester batting

Light brown, brown, and light blue thread

Fusible web

½ yard (45.7 cm) brown cotton

SEAM ALLOWANCE

¼ inch (6 mm)

FINISHED SIZE

10 x 14¾ inches
(25.4 x 37.5 cm) each

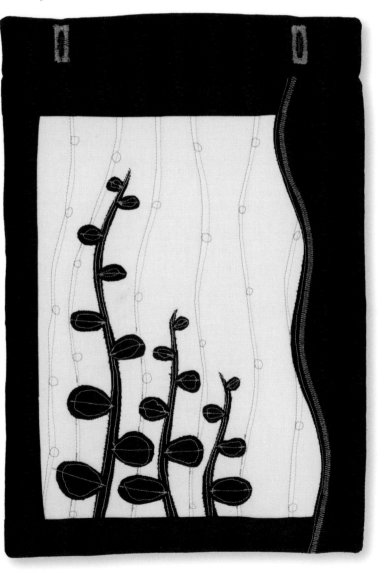

$\mathcal{T}$endrils of brown kelp stretch upward on this two-panel quilt. The two buttonholes in each part let you devise whatever hanging method you'd like.

WHAT YOU DO

1 To make one panel of the quilt, cut the cream fabric to 8½ x 11½ inches (21.6 x 29.2 cm) and place it face up on a 10½ x 13½-inch (26.7 x 34.3 cm) piece of batting. Pin-baste the layers together at the corners.

2 Stitch the layers together, creating wavy lines with light brown thread and spacing the lines about 1 inch (2.5 cm) apart. Switch to light blue thread and stitch next to the light brown lines, stopping every 2 inches (5.1 cm) to disengage the walker foot and making a free-motion circle over the light brown stitch lines.

3 Draw three kelp stalks— 9½ inches (24.1 cm), 5½ inches (14 cm), and 4 inches (10.2 cm) tall—and leaves onto

DESIGNER

AMANDA CARESTIO

the paper side of the fusible web. Fuse the web to the wrong side of the brown cotton and then cut out the shapes. Iron the shapes in place, over the stitch lines, on the quilt top.

4 Using light brown thread, stitch along the stalks with two lines of straight stitches and around the inside of each leaf with free-motion stitches. Create a straight line of stitching down the center of each leaf.

5 Cut 1½-inch (3.8 cm) wide strips of brown cotton to the following lengths: one at 13½ inches (34.3 cm) and two at 8½ inches (21.6 cm). Attach the borders around the outside of the cream fabric, starting with the long edge (next to the tallest kelp stalk) and then the shorter top and bottom edges.

6 Cut a piece of fusible web-backed brown cotton that measures 3 x 13½ inches (7.6 x 34.3 cm). Cut one long side to create a curved edge and fuse it in place on the quilt top (next to the shortest kelp stalk) over the other border pieces.

7 To create the hanging tab, cut two pieces of brown fabric to 2½ x 10½ inches (6.4 x 26.7 cm). Pin the pieces together with right sides facing and stitch along the edges, leaving one long edge open. Turn the tab right side out and create two buttonholes about 2 inches (5.1 cm) in from each outside edge using the light blue thread.

8 Cut a piece of brown cotton to 10½ x 13½ inches (26.7 x 34.3 cm) for the backing. Stack the layers in the following order: batting (which has already been attached to the quilt top), the quilt top face down, and the backing face up. Sandwich the tab between the quilt top and the backing so the top raw edges are aligned.

9 Pin the layers together along the edges and stitch along each edge, leaving a 4-inch (10.2 cm) slit unstitched for turning.

10 Clip the seam allowances and the corners. Turn the quilt inside out through the slit, and stitch along the edges of the quilt (not the tab) with the brown thread, sewing the slit closed.

11 Stitch along the curved border edge, using light blue thread with a zigzag stitch and light brown thread with a straight stitch.

12 Repeat steps 1 through 11 to create the second panel, placing the kelp on the quilt top in the opposite order as the first panel.

ONE QUILT AT A TIME (OR TWO)

You can create one panel first and then the other, as the instructions indicate. Or you could do both at the same time by simply doing each step twice. One advantage of the second method is efficiency in cutting out similar pieces; one disadvantage is that you might learn a thing or two from making the first panel that could help you while making the second.

portrait of Velma

*Y*ou may think you're a quilter and not a portrait painter. Follow the simple techniques here and suddenly you're both.

DESIGNER

SUSAN LEWIS STOREY

WHAT YOU NEED

Basic Quilting Tool Kit (page 11)

Photograph

Computer with digital imaging software, or copy machine

Scanner and printer

Fabric treatment for making computer-printed fabrics washable

½ yard (45.7 cm) white cotton

½ yard (45.7 cm) contact paper

½ yard (45.7 cm) black cotton

Low-loft batting, 13 x 18 inches (33 x 45.7 cm)

Variegated quilting thread

Embellishments, such as buttons, beads, and decorative brads

Beading needle and thread

Embroidery thread and needle

SEAM ALLOWANCE

None

FINISHED SIZE

12 x 17 inches (30.5 x 43.2 cm)

WHAT YOU DO

1 Scan the photograph you're recreating with photo imaging software and resize the image to your desired dimensions. This portrait of Susan Lewis Storey's grandmother was resized to 12 x 17 inches (30.5 x 43.2 cm). Digitally correct any imperfections, and adjust the black-and-white balance of the photo. Add the outlines using a "posterization" filter to create the whimsical cartoon drawing effect.

2 To make the quilt without any digital imaging, start instead with this simpler photocopy method. Take the original photo to a local copy center, adjust the size and light/dark balance, print a black-and-white paper copy, color this by hand, and outline it as desired. Then scan that image into the computer before moving on to step 3.

3 Treat the white fabric with the fabric treatment according to its directions, air dry, and iron. Attach the treated white fabric to the contact paper, being careful to eliminate any wrinkling or bubbling. Cut the fabric and paper to the appropriate size for your printer.

4 Print the image onto the fabric. Remove the contact paper, then rinse, air dry, and iron the fabric.

5 Trim the black fabric to slightly larger than the batting. Layer the batting between the print and the black backing fabric. Using variegated thread, free-motion quilt the entire piece, then trim to size.

6 Cut 1½ yards (1.4 m) of black fabric strips 1½ inches (3.8 cm) wide for binding, and bind the quilt.

7 Embellish with a variety of beads, buttons, and embroidery to accent the image.

8 From the remaining black fabric, cut and attach a sleeve to the back for hanging.

SIZING IT UP

If you're able to use a large-format printer that will print up to the size of this quilt image—great! If you only have a standard printer, though, you can adjust the size of your project to suit your printer, or print opposite halves of your image on two separate sheets of fabric. Allow for a slight overlap on each print, then piece the halves together to create the size you want.

spring haiku

Colorful fabrics and some sweet embellishments make a lovely quilt.

Warm days and cool nights.
Life begins its flow to roots.
Joy is in the air.

DESIGNER

KATHY DANIELS

WHAT YOU NEED

Basic Quilting Tool Kit (page 11)

¼ yard (22.9 cm) each of 5 or 6 different green cotton fabrics

¼ yard (22.9 cm) yellow cotton fabric

¼ yard (22.9 cm) varied cotton fabrics for flowers

½ yard (45.7 cm) fusible web

Fine-point marker

½ yard (45.7 cm) cotton batting

½ yard (45.7 cm) backing material

Yellow embroidery thread

Beads to embellish (your choice)

¼ yard (22.9 cm) black-and-white cotton fabric

SEAM ALLOWANCE

¼ inch (6 mm)

FINISHED SIZE

16 x 14 inches (40.6 x 35.6 cm)

WHAT YOU DO

1 Cut five strips of green fabric measuring 16½ inches (41.9 cm) long by varying widths to equal 8¼ inches (21 cm) when sewn together with ¼ inch (6 mm) seam allowances. Cut the yellow fabric to measure 16½ x 6¼ inches (41.9 x 15.9 cm). Strip-piece the greens together and sew them to the upper yellow piece. Press flat.

2 Choose your fabrics for flowers and stems, and iron fusible web to each back. Trace an oval pattern onto the paper backing of the fusible web, cut out two oval flower tops, and pin them to the right side of the yellow top. This will guide where to place your haiku.

3 Print out the words of the haiku shown here (or your own) from a computer, testing to find a font and size you like. Position your printed paper under the yellow background fabric and put it on top of a light box, tape it to a window, or (if you can see the letters well enough) just leave it on the table. Trace it lightly in pencil and, when you're sure of the design, go over the letters with a fine-point marking pen to make it easier to see. This will be covered with thread.

4 Assemble your quilt sandwich—quilt top, batting, backing—and baste well. Use a dark thread to begin machine quilting your letters one at a time. Go very slowly, cutting threads as you go. Go over each letter about three times before moving on to the next. Hint: If this seems difficult to you, try a practice piece first.

5 When the script is done, quilt the lower section very simply by using a running stitch along the seams.

6 Cut out your flowers and stems freehand and position them to your liking. Iron them in place. Stitch with coordinating

thread colors around the flowers, leaves, and stems. The ferns were stitched using a free-motion zig-zag, but you could also do them with a regular machine zigzag.

7 Use a pencil to lightly sketch some lines to represent air currents through the yellow background. Hand-quilt these lines with two strands of yellow embroidery floss.

8 Embellish the edges of the oval flowers by using a but-tonhole stitch to apply medium-sized beads. Embellish with small beads on the tops of the other flowers and anywhere else you like.

9 Bind the edges with the black-and-white fabric. If you wish, use the same fabric to sew a sleeve onto the top of the back of the quilt for hanging.

WHAT YOU NEED

Basic Quilting Tool Kit (page 11)

Template (page 138)

Bleached muslin, 10 x 12 inches
(25.4 x 30.5 cm)

Light box (optional)

Sandpaper board (optional)

Wax pastels in gold, pale yellow,
salmon pink, purple, moss green,
orangish yellow, lemon yellow,
bright yellow, and ochre

Artist's paintbrush

Parchment paper

Fan brush

Cup of water and paper towel

Low-loft cotton batting, 9 x 11
inches (22.9 x 27.9 cm)

Sheet of stabilizer, 9 x 11 inches
(22.9 x 27.9 cm)

Black embroidery thread

Brown variegated embroidery
thread

Cotton backing, 10 x 12 inches
(25.4 x 30.5 cm)

DESIGNER

FANNIE NARTE

whimsical rose

*T*his happy marriage of a watercolor painting and an art quilt
combines delicate lines and shadings into a beautiful whole.

SEAM ALLOWANCE

None

FINISHED SIZE

8 x 10 inches (20.3 x 25.4 cm)

WHAT YOU DO

1 Copy the template on page 138. Place the template onto a light box or tape it on a sunny window. Place the muslin quilt top piece onto the line drawing and trace the lines with a water-soluble fabric pen.

2 Place the quilt top onto the sandpaper board or a piece of cardboard. With the paintbrush, lightly paint the wax pastels on the quilt top, following the project photo.

3 Place the quilt top onto the parchment paper. Dip the fan brush into the cup of water, tap the brush on the rim to remove excess water, and blend each of the color segments using circular motions, repeating as necessary. Blend geometric shapes of the

background first. Next, blend the rose, stem, and leaves. (For best results, use water sparingly. Rinse the brush in clean water before moving to a new area of color.)

4 Review the painted quilt top. You may want to add more color to certain areas, or else lighten the color in places by applying water with your fan brush and blotting the area with a paper towel. When you're pleased with your quilt top, leave it on the parchment paper and let it air dry for two to three hours.

5 Place a clean sheet of parchment paper larger than your quilt top onto your ironing surface. Place your quilt top face down onto the parchment paper. Add another piece of parchment paper on top of the quilt top to protect the iron's surface. Use the medium heat setting and iron.

6 Turn the quilt top right side up and place it onto parchment paper. Add another piece of parchment paper to the quilt top and iron as in step 5.

7 If your line drawing has disappeared, retrace the lines following the directions in step 1.

8 Insert the batting between the quilt top and the sheet of stabilizer. Pin-baste the quilt sandwich, including the backing. Turn the quilt sandwich over, wrong side up, and baste a scant 1/16 inch (1.6 mm) in from the edge, using black embroidery thread.

9 Drop the feed dogs. Thread sketch each geometric shape two to three times, using brown variegated embroidery thread. Then thread sketch the rose, stem, and leaves two to three times, using black embroidery thread.

10 Trim the excess fabric. Fuse the quilt backing to the quilt and trim its excess fabric.

11 To finish the quilt, satin stitch the edges with black embroidery thread.

HOLD IT RIGHT THERE

What's that sandpaper board mentioned in step 2? You can make one yourself by gluing a piece of medium-rough sandpaper to each inside part of a folder. Open the folder, lay it on your table, and you've got a slightly rough surface that can hold fabric in place as you work on it.

$\mathscr{Y}$*hop* in your step

ou can never be too old (or young) to enjoy seeing a simple and charming scene hanging on the bedroom wall.

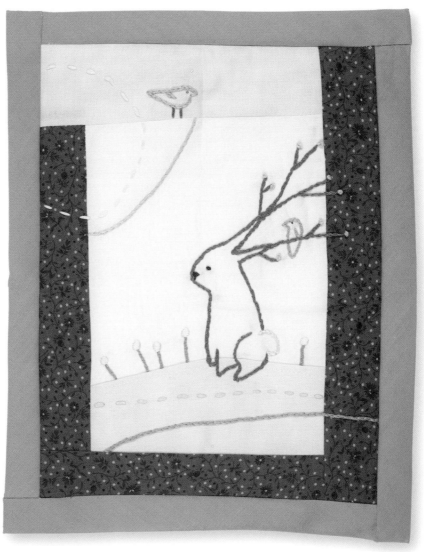

WHAT YOU NEED

Basic Quilting Tool Kit (page 11)

Light green cotton, one piece 8 x 3 inches (20.3 x 7.6 cm) and one piece 7 x 3 inches (17.8 x 7.6 cm)

Dark green cotton in these sizes: 10 x 2½ inches (25.4 x 6.4 cm), 12 x 2½ inches (30.5 x 6.4 cm), and 8 x 2½ inches (20.3 x 6.4 cm)

White cotton, one piece 7 x 9 inches (17.8 x 22.9 cm) and one piece 9½ x 12 inches (22.9 x 30.5 cm)

Embroidery floss in light green, dark green, brown, light brown, cream, and white

Batting, 9½ x 12 inches (24.1 x 30.5 cm)

Green bias tape, two 11-inch (27.9 cm) and two 14-inch (35.6 cm) pieces

SEAM ALLOWANCE

¼ inch (6 mm)

FINISHED SIZE

9½ x 12 inches (24.1 x 30.5 cm)

WHAT YOU DO

1 To make the front quilt piece, sew together the two light green and three dark green piece with the 7 x 9 inch (17.8 x 22.9 cm) white piece as shown in the photo. You'll need to cut a curve along the top of the shorter light green piece to make the hilltop.

2 Draw lines for the embroidery pattern with a fabric marker onto the quilt front and embroider the design with the floss.

3 Sandwich the quilt front, batting, and remaining 9½ x 12-inch (22.9 x 30.5 cm) white piece together and pin with safety pins, starting in the center. Quilt the layers together using the tying method, with bits of embroidery floss to match the fabric colors on the front. Make the knots at the back.

4 Sew the bias tape around the edge, folding in the corners.

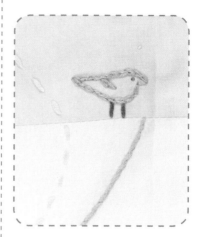

DESIGNER

AIMEE RAY

teahouse visit

*H*ere's a fun quilt with framing to hang in your breakfast nook or dining room, or next to your favorite reading chair.

WHAT YOU NEED

Basic Quilting Tool Kit (page 11)

2 yards (1.8 m) of 1½-inch (3.8 cm) x ½-inch (1.3 cm) wood strips

Handsaw and miter box

Wood glue

Staple gun and staples

¾ yard (68.6 cm) pale muslin or cotton

4 scraps of white fabrics in different textures, such as gauze, linen, cotton, silk, or white chiffon

¼ yard (22.9 cm) fabric in a hot pink pattern

Scrap of lace

White rickrack

Glue stick

Double-sided paper-backed fusible web

6 fat quarters in print colors from green to turquoise blue

Tea bag

Scrap of sheer fabric for the front of the tea bag

Green felt scrap

Embroidery floss in medium blue, light blue, pale green, gray, and hot pink

Fabric glue

Embroidery needle

Marking pen

4 large white buttons

4 medium-size hot pink buttons

¾ yard (68.6 cm) cotton print for backing

Hammer

1 large-size picture-frame hanger

SEAM ALLOWANCE

Varies

FINISHED SIZE

13 x 20¼ inches (33 x 51.4 cm)

WHAT YOU DO

MAKING THE FRAME

1 Cut the wood strips in a miter box with the following lengths and angles. See figure 1 for an indication of what the pieces will look like. (Note: All lengths are for the longer edge of the strip after cutting at an angle.)

- 1 bottom board: 12½ inches (31.8 cm) long with 45° angles on each end

- 2 sides: each 13¾ inches (35 cm) long with a 45° angle at the bottom and 22.5° angle at the top

- 2 roof pieces: each 8⅞ inches (22.5 cm) long with a 22.5° angle on the bottom end and a 45° angle at the top

DESIGNER

ALYSSE HENNESSEY

2 Lay the wood strips out on your rotary cutting board grid, and line everything up with straight angles (figure 1 again). Put a fat drop of wood glue on each end and press the ends together to make the same alignment. Staple twice across each corner, then flip the frame and staple each corner again.

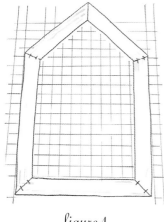

figure 1

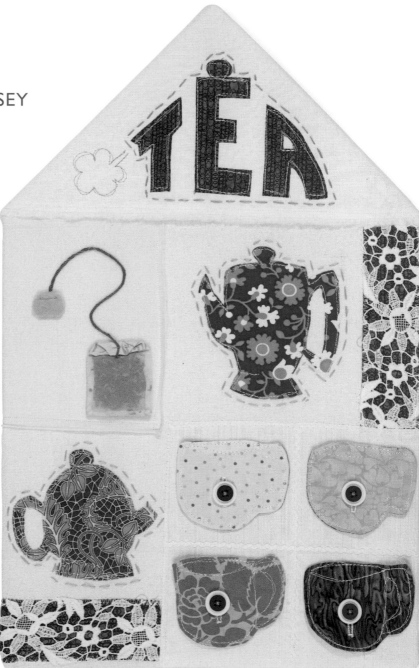

3 Lay the wood frame on the muslin and trace around the outside with a pencil. Draw a second outline 4 inches (10.2 cm) outside of the first and cut along this line. Set the frame aside.

4 Draw a horizontal line with a water-soluble fabric marker across the muslin to form a triangle for the roof. Draw a vertical and a horizontal line within the large square below the roof to create four uneven quadrants similar to the layout shown here.

5 Try out your four scraps of white fabrics in different combinations over the muslin. Decide which to use in the different quadrants and on the roof, and which edges to finish, leave unfinished, or overlap. Cut the pieces to fit and pin in place over the muslin. Flip the entire top over and trim off all fabric to match the far edges of the muslin pattern. Lay the wood frame on top again and trace around it with the fabric marker.

6 Cut two 2-inch (5.1 cm) wide strips of the hot pink fabric to lay out on the edge of two of the quadrants. Cover the strips with lace. Tuck the strips under the white fabric quadrants and pin in place.

7 Divide the lower right quadrant into four smaller sections with white rickrack. Use a glue stick to hold the rickrack in place and let it dry before sewing. Stitch down all edges of the pieces on the quilt top, using a combination of straight stitch and zigzag, with double lines of stitching. Stitch down the edges of the lace with a zigzag stitch.

NO CARPENTER REQUIRED

Maybe the woodworking here is making you say, "Hey, I signed up for home ec, not shop class." Don't sweat it! Just buy standard-sized strips from a home-improvement or craft store in an easy-to-cut wood like pine. If you don't have a miter box, just mark the angles in pencil with a protractor, and saw on the lines as well as you can. The quilt top will cover up all your carpentry work—expert or otherwise—anyway.

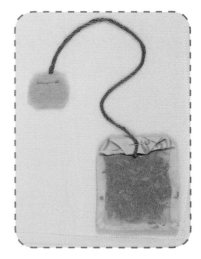

8 Lay a piece of double-sided paper-backed fusible web on the roof and lightly trace the roof shape to see how much room you have to form the teakettle. Pull open a corner of the paper to find out which side will come off first, leaving the sticky on the other side. The easy-to-remove side is the top surface to draw on.

9 Sketch the outline of the steaming teakettle onto the fusible web. Cut out this shape. You will later form the outside of the kettle in embroidery, so lay it on the quilt and trace the outside edge with a fabric pen. Draw a burst of steam coming out of the end. Back on the fusible web, draw the letters T-E-A to fill the shape of the kettle, and a knob bump on top of letter E (see the project photo).

10 Cut out the letters T-E-A and remove the top surface paper. Stick the letters to the back side of the pink fabric. Press firmly and cut out again. Your fabric letters should be right side up and facing the right direction when laid out on the quilt. Remove the paper backing and stick the letters firmly into place. When all looks good, iron them onto the quilt following the manufacturer's instructions.

11 Use the same technique as in steps 8 to 10 to create the two teapots from other print fabrics. Instead of in the roof space, place the teapots in two of the quadrants.

12 Look at a tea bag and examine the way it is constructed and folded together. Recreate the tea bag using the reverse side of the light green cotton print for the back of the bag and a sheer scrap for the front. Cut a length of medium blue embroidery floss for the string, and a piece of green felt for the tag. Use real tea to fill the tea bag halfway and staple it closed like a real tea bag. Finish the tea bag by gluing it to the quilt top in one of the quadrants, with a fun curve in the string.

BEAUTIFUL AND FRAGRANT

You can use the actual tea from your tea bag model in this quilt, or choose whatever other sweet-smelling, long-lasting material—crushed potpourri or dried lavender buds, perhaps?—you'd like.

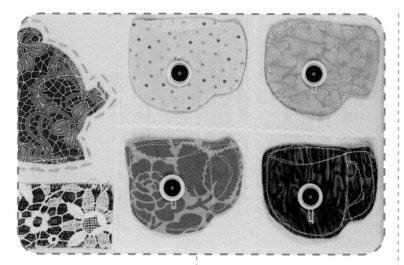

16 Lay the teacups in their squares to plan out button placement. Make the buttonholes big enough to fit the double-stacked buttons through. Stitch a buttonhole on each teacup, then cut them open. Lay the cups on the quilt again, and mark the top end of the buttonhole on the quilt so you can see where to stitch the button on. Stitch on the stacked white and pink buttons with hot pink embroidery floss.

ASSEMBLING THE QUILT

17 Lay out the quilt face down, with the frame lined up properly on top. Mark all the corners right onto the back with a pencil. Mark the quilt back 1½ inches (3.8 cm) wider than the frame with ruler and pencil. Cut the excess fabric off. Finish the edge with a wide zigzag that wraps around the edge.

13 Embroider the quilt with a needle big enough to handle all six strands of the embroidery floss. Make big, bold stitches to go around both teapots (green embroidery floss) and the teakettle (light blue floss). Embroider the kettle's steam in smaller gray stitches and three strands of the embroidery floss.

14 Use a piece of sturdy paper and a pencil to sketch a pattern for your teacups. The teacups will need to fit in the squares formed by rickrack in step 7. Finalize your line with a marking pen, and add a ¼-inch (6 mm) seam allowance. Cut out the pattern.

15 The four teacups are reversible, so pick one print for the front of each and another for the back. Lay the light green, dark green, light blue, and dark blue fabrics face down on their backing fabrics. Reverse the cup pattern, and pin and trace it onto each cup in turn. Sew around each cup edge, leaving an opening at the cup's bottom to turn the fabric. Clip notches in the curves of the seam allowance. Turn right side out, and press smooth with a steam iron. Topstitch simple details on the right side of the cup with white thread. This will also close the opening.

18 Line the quilt back with a cotton print and cut off anything that sticks beyond the frame. Use a few drops of glue to hold the backing in place. Add a label if you like. Put the wooden frame on the quilt back, using your pencil marks to get the placement right.

19 Staple the quilt in place, as you would hang a painter's canvas. Start on one side and add a staple. Go to the opposite side, stretch it a bit, and staple. Staple the top, pulling very gently until the quilt is more attached to the frame. Stretch and staple the bottom edge. Keep working the opposite sides, pulling taut until it's all in place and the corners are folded smooth. Tap all the staples with a hammer to settle them into the wood. Hammer in the picture-frame hanger at the top, just below where the fabric is stapled.

in a doll's house

*I*t's the luckiest doll in any child's bedroom that gets to sleep under a quilt made with this luxurious silk dupioni and sophisticated trapunto technique.

WHAT YOU NEED

Basic Quilting Tool Kit (page 11)

Plain cotton for backing, 13-inch (33 cm) square

Heat-transfer pencil or fabric pencil or pen

Lilac silk dupioni, two 13-inch (33 cm) squares

Variegated embroidery thread for quilting

Wool roving in natural cream

Tapestry needle and tweezers (optional)

Organic cotton batting, 13-inch (33 cm) square

Knitting needle

Hand-quilting thread in lilac

SEAM ALLOWANCE

Varies

FINISHED SIZE

11½ inches (29.2 cm) square

DESIGNER

RUTH SINGER

WHAT YOU DO

1 Draw a template for a set of three oval shapes. Each shape should be about 2½ x 1¼ inches (6.4 x 3.2 cm), as in the actual-size photo below right. Trace the design four times onto the plain cotton fabric, either using a heat-transfer pencil or tracing directly onto the cotton.

2 Put one square of silk dupioni face down and place the plain cotton square on top. Pin and baste the piece around the edges and in a cross to keep the layers from moving around.

3 Start stitching each oval design by fastening the embroidery thread in the backing fabric, just outside the marked stitching line. Stitch around the outlines of each design with a small running stitch, taking care to keep the stitches even on the underside, which will be the finished front. Remove the basting when all the stitching is complete. Press the stitched quilt top.

4 In the areas to be stuffed (the larger parts of the oval and not the smaller circles), separate the front and back layers by pinching the fabrics between finger and thumb. Cut two small holes in the backing fabric only, at the top of the egg shape and again at the narrowest part.

5 Use small pieces of wool roving to stuff the space. You will need to use tiny pieces and a blunt tapestry needle to stuff the very narrow areas. Using very pointed tweezers may help. Do not overstuff, as it will cause the fabric to pucker around the stitching. Sew up the holes neatly.

6 When the entire design is quilted, place the quilt top faceup, the quilt backing face down on top, and the quilt batting on the very top. Machine-sew all around the quilt using a ⅝-inch (1.6 cm) seam allowance and leaving 3 inches (7.6 cm) open on one side.

7 Trim the seam allowances by about half, and clip the corners. Turn the quilt through the open gap and gently push the corners out using a knitting needle. Fold under the seam allowances in the opening and hand-sew closed. Press the edges of the quilt, avoiding the quilted area.

8 Using matching hand-quilting thread, stitch around the edge of the quilt, about ⅝ inch (1.6 cm) in from the edge.

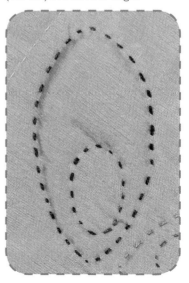

95

dress shop memories

*T*his quilt recreates the history of those women who worked every day making beautiful and useful things out of whole cloth.

DESIGNER

JANET COOPER

WHAT YOU NEED

Basic Quilting Tool Kit (page 11)

1 yard (.9 m) burlap, buckram, or other sturdy backing fabric

1 yard (.9 m) colorful fabric to go between the quilt top and backing

Recycled fabrics, such as old tablecloths, nightgowns, bedspreads, flowered handkerchiefs, dish towels, and bits of lace and netting

Papers, such as wallpaper scraps, comic strips, old magazine images, handwritten pages, sewing patterns, or tissue papers

Embellishments, such as buttons, jewelry parts, sewing accessories, little toys, and photographs

4 yards (3.7 m) trim or band lace

Leather and doll-making needles

Yarn darners

Sturdy button thread

Embroidery thread

1 yard (.9 m) of ball chain for the bottom hem

Heavy cardboard and glue (optional)

SEAM ALLOWANCE

None

FINISHED SIZE

22 x 32 inches (55.9 x 81.3 cm)

WHAT YOU DO

1 Make a template for the shape of the entire quilt from a sheet of newspaper or wrapping paper. Cut the backing fabric and the colorful fabric from the template. Baste them together with large stitches around the edge.

2 Assemble your palette of cloths and papers and begin by assembling a dozen or so squares and rectangles of contrasting fabrics. Use simple stitches to attach the layers of fabrics and objects into five vertical panels.

3 Arrange these panels on your backing and attach with simple hand stitches. Use cloth or paper to make the shoulders of the dress and attach.

4 Fashion a few dolls from layers of tissue, netting, or cloth and attach them to the quilt. Highlight the panels with stitches and lace.

5 Sew a chain of lace onto the hem of the dress. Create a ruffle from tissue and attach it as a collar. Using netting and tissue, twist and create flowers for the bottom border.

6 If you wish to hang up the piece, attach a piece of heavy cardboard to the top part of the back of the piece with glue. Add a loop through the cardboard at each shoulder to hang the dress.

elephants in the garden

Elegant restraint is nice for some quilts, but sometimes—like here—
you just want to create something exuberant and exotic.

DESIGNER

ANDI STERN

WHAT YOU NEED

Basic Quilting Tool Kit (page 11)

3 fat quarters of assorted dark blue cottons

3 fat quarters of assorted light blue cottons

3 fat quarters of assorted medium blue cottons

3 fat quarters of assorted green cottons (in addition to the green fabrics listed below)

1 yard (.9 m) patterned cotton for backing and sleeve

½ yard (45.7 cm) batting

½ yard (45.7 cm) dark red cotton

1½ yards (1.4 m) interfacing

⅛ yard (11.4 cm) scraps of dupioni silk or other fancy fabric in light cream, deep yellow, and orange

⅛ yard (11.4 cm) patterned cotton for the ears

1 fat quarter of brown fabric such as batik

Furry brown yarn

Blue cotton fabric for binding, 9 x 44 inches (22.9 x 111.7 cm)

1 fat quarter of light green cotton or silk

1 fat quarter of dark green cotton or silk

1 skein embroidery floss for the grass

2 skeins embroidery floss for the sky

Red gimp for couching around the elephant body

Dark red braid for ears and blankets

6 x 24-inch (15.2 x 61 cm) scrap of brown fabric for the dates

Small pieces of polyester stuffing for the dates

12 12-mm mother-of-pearl discs

2 12-mm dark brown buttons

2 20-mm mother-of-pearl buttons

6 20-mm red buttons

4 30-mm dentallium shells

Beading needle and thread

Machine threads for quilting and piecework

SEAM ALLOWANCE

¼ inch (6 mm)

FINISHED SIZE

36 x 18 inches (91.4 x 45.7 cm)

WHAT YOU DO

1 Using a rotary cutter and cutting mat, cut 100 1 x 3-inch (2.5 x 7.6 cm) strips of the dark blue fabrics. Sew the strips together on the long side to make a block that is five strips wide. Repeat to make 20 blocks. Press the blocks.

2 Sew the blocks together, alternating the directions of the strips in the blocks; make five strips of four blocks each. Press the strips and trim the excess fabric so that the blocks are straight. Sew the strips together so that you have a finished block that is five blocks high by four blocks wide. Press and trim.

3 Repeat steps 1 and 2 with the medium blues, then repeat them again with the light blues.

4 Cut 120 1 x 3-inch (2.5 x 7.6 cm) strips of the assorted greens. Follow steps 1 and 2 again, only this time you will make 24 blocks. Press the blocks and sew together two strips of 12 blocks each, alternating the direction the long side goes. Sew the two long strips together and press.

5 Sew the blue blocks together, going from left to right with dark, medium, and light blues. Press. Sew the green strip to the bottom of the blue blocks. Press the entire top.

6 Lay out your backing fabric wrong side up, layer that with the batting, then lay the quilt top on top, right side up. Pin together and stitch to outline the quilt.

7 Draw or trace an elephant pattern and cut it out. Trace two elephant patterns onto the interfacing, flipping it over to make one that faces right and one that faces left. Pin the interfacing to the dark red fabric, wrong sides together. Sew the elephants to the fabric, following the lines you traced. Trim the excess fabric and interfacing, leaving the elephant shapes.

8 Pin the elephants to your quilt. Use a ruler to help with placement, as your backing is currently a little larger than the 36-inch (91.4 cm) width of the finished piece. Use a zigzag stitch to attach them to the quilt.

9 Draw a blanket pattern and trace two of them to the interfacing in the same way you did the elephants. Follow the rest of steps 7 and 8, using the orange fancy fabric, and sew the blankets to the elephants. Do the same to make the elephant ears with the patterned cotton.

10 Draw a tree pattern, create a tree in the same manner as above with the brown batik fabric, and sew it to the quilt. Couch the brown yarn to the tree at 1½ to 2-inch (3.8 to 5.1 cm) intervals.

11 Cut the 9 x 44-inch (22.9 x 111.7 cm) length of blue fabric into four equal pieces, each about 2 x 44 inches (5.1 x 111.7 cm). Bind the edges of the quilt.

12 Draw or trace a leaf pattern and trace it six times onto the interfacing.

13 Cut the light and dark green cottons into 3-inch (7.6 cm) long strips and sew them together to make a larger 6-inch (15.2 cm) wide piece of striped fabric.

14 Place the striped fabric right sides together with a solid piece of fabric and lay that onto a piece of batting, with the solid fabric facing up. Lay one of the interfacing leaves onto that and sew. Trim the leaf and turn it out. Repeat five more times, to make a total of six leaves. Press the leaves.

15 Sew around the outside and center vein of the leaves with a contrasting thread.

16 Cross-stitch the background of the quilt by hand, using complementary colors of embroidery floss for the sky and the grass.

17 Using the gimp, couch around the outside of the elephants. Using the braid and a cotton thread, stab stitch around the blankets and ears on the elephants.

18 Fuse a scrap of the cream and golden yellow silks to the interfacing and draw a sun and moon onto the paper. Fuse the sun and moon to the quilt.

19 Pin the leaves to the tree and machine sew them to the quilt with contrasting thread.

20 Press the scrap of brown fabric, folding it along the long side for the dates. Draw three fat oval shapes onto the fabric with a pencil, then sew around the shape, leaving the tops open. Turn the dates and stuff them with the polyester stuffing. Sew the dates closed and sew them to the center of the tree.

21 Embellish the elephant by sewing the mother-of-pearl discs to the feet. Sew the elephants' eyes on by placing the brown buttons on top of the white mother-of-pearl buttons and sewing them both on. Sew three red buttons on each blanket. Sew on the dentallium shell tusks by stringing one shell, then the other, pushing them together to make a long tusk and sewing back into the quilt. Secure the tusk further by sewing over the shells in three places.

22 Cut a piece of backing fabric 8 x 36 inches (20.3 x 91.4 cm). Fold over the short ends of the fabric and sew.

23 Fold the sleeve in half long sides together and press. Unfold the sleeve and fold the long sides into the pressed line. Press. Pin the sleeve to the back of the quilt, about 1 inch (2.5 cm) from the top and 1 inch (2.5 cm) from either side. Using a whipstitch, sew the sleeve to the back of the quilt. If desired, make a label and sew it to the back of the quilt. Use a dowel or thin wooden piece to create a hanging bar.

ANOTHER NOTCH IN YOUR QUILT

Sometimes you need perfectly straight lines, and sometimes you don't. When making strips for binding (as in step 11) or for the sleeve (step 22), you can just make notches on the edge of your bigger piece, each separated by the approximate width you need, and rip the strips.

spanish flowers

DESIGNER

CINDY COOKSEY

*T*he hexagons in this geometric quilt allow you to create what seems like 50 *really* little mini quilts, each with its own unique combination of fabric, stitching, and embellishment.

WHAT YOU NEED

Basic Quilting Tool Kit (page 11)

Sheets of paper hexagon templates, with each side of the hexagon 1 inch (2.5 cm) long

25 pieces of cotton fabric, each at least 3 x 6 inches (7.6 x 15.2 cm), in red, magenta, orange, yellow, green, blue green, blue, and purple

Batting, 13 x 15 inches (33 x 38.1 cm)

Cotton fabric for backing, 13 x 15 inches (33 x 38.1 cm)

Beads, buttons, and other embellishments (such as shisha mirrors)

SEAM ALLOWANCE

¼ inch (6 mm)

FINISHED SIZE

12 x 14 inches (30.5 x 35.6 cm)

WHAT YOU DO

1 Cut out 50 paper hexagon templates. (Note: You can create printable hexagon templates in any size you choose for free at online sites such as www. incompetech.com/graphpaper/hexagonal.) Pin a template on the wrong side of one of your 25 fabric pieces, leaving room to put another template on the other half of the piece. Cut the fabric around the template, leaving a ¼ inch (6 mm) seam allowance. Repeat until you have created 50 fabric hexagons (two from each fabric piece), each pinned with a template (figure 1).

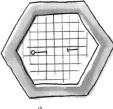

figure 1

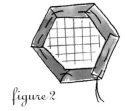

figure 2

2 For each hexagon, turn over the seam allowance on each edge, and baste the seam allowances down (figure 2).

3 Start arranging the 50 hexagons in a pleasing pattern, leaving open spaces as in the quilt pictured here. To begin sewing the hexagons together, place two of them right sides together. Whipstitch one edge down, using tiny stitches in a matching thread so they won't be too noticeable. Try to avoid sewing into the paper templates. Knot at the end of the edge and cut the thread. Open the hexagons out to show two side-by-side hexagons.

4 Place another hexagon onto one of the attached hexagons, right sides together, and whipstitch as before. Continue until you have completed the top row of six hexagons. Keep the paper templates attached to the hexagons until instructed to remove them.

5 Make the second row of hexagons the same as the first, except with seven hexagons. Continue making rows of hexagons, alternating six or seven in each row, until you have five rows. Referring to the photo of the quilt, sew together shorter rows of two or three hexagons to allow for the gaps in between.

6 Begin sewing the rows to each other, starting with the top two rows. As before, place right sides together, one edge at a time, securing the corners with an extra stitch or two. You'll need to fold adjacent hexagons out of the way as you sew each edge. After

you've sewn all the rows together as in the quilt photo, press them with an iron on a cotton setting. Carefully remove the basting threads and then all the paper hexagon templates. (They can be used again for other projects.) Keep the seam allowances folded in place.

7 Pin the batting to the back of the quilt top, with pins on the right side of the quilt top. Use one pin in each of the outer hexagons and at least some of the inner hexagons. Carefully cut the batting to exactly the same shape as the top, following the angles of each hexagon and cutting out the three holes with no hexagons.

8 Pin the backing fabric to the back of the quilt, with the right side facing out. As you place new pins into the quilt sandwich, you may remove the old pins that had secured the batting. Carefully cut the backing as you did the batting.

9 Fold the seam allowance of the backing so that it folds over the batting edge and the seam allowance slips between the batting and the quilt top. You'll need to clip the seam allowance of the backing fabric at the inner corners, taking care not to clip too far in. Blind-stitch the backing fabric to the quilt top, securing the inner and outer corners with an extra stitch or two. Use the same process to finish the three holes.

10 Remove the pins. Quilt each hexagon shape as desired. This quilt uses a spiral quilting design for most hexagons, with some having spokes in a starburst design.

11 Embellish the center of each hexagon with beads, buttons, or shisha mirrors.

12 Prepare for hanging by adding a standard quilt sleeve on the top half of the backing, using the remaining fabric of your choice.

DASH TO YOUR STASH

Think of this quilt as a chance to use just about any embellishment in your collection—from seed, bugle, ladybug, and butterfly beads to heart, flower, and leaf buttons. The tiny round shisha mirror included (see the middle of the detail photo below) is an example of an Indian embroidery technique that originally used pieces of mica to add shiny reflections to fabric work.

have a cup

DESIGNER

MARY HUBBARD

*D*o you know someone who loves to sip tea out in the garden? Have we got a quilt to make for her!

WHAT YOU NEED

Basic Quilting Tool Kit (page 11)

1 sheet quilt of template plastic at least 5 x 5 inches (12.7 x 12.7 cm)

Silver quilt-marking pencil

⅛ yard (11.4 cm) cotton print for teacup

⅛ yard (11.4 cm) blue cotton for inside of cup

⅛ yard (11.4 cm) synthetic fur in pink/red for petals

⅛ yard (11.4 cm) green polyester or wool felt for leaves

1 fat quarter of cotton for background

Embroidery, chenille, quilt basting, and beading needles

Yellow and red perle cotton

Light green silk embroidery ribbon, 4 mm wide

1 fat quarter of cotton for backing

1 fat quarter of cotton batting

1 full skein of variegated blue-green embroidery floss

⅛ yard (11.4 cm) cotton fabric for binding

White beading thread

Twisted silver-lined bugle beads in chartreuse, size 5

About 32 sequins in different colors and varieties, including clear rainbow and metallic

Seed beads in cranberry luster, size 11

Metallic iris bugle beads in brown, size 1

Charlotte beads in purple iris AB, size 13

SEAM ALLOWANCE

Varies

FINISHED SIZE

8⅜ inches (21.3 cm) square

WHAT YOU DO

1 Use a pencil to draw or trace pattern pieces onto the plastic template sheet for the following: cup, cup handle, inside of cup, petal, and leaf. Cut out the templates. Using the templates and the silver quilt pencil, trace the cup, cup handle, and the inside of the cup on the right side of your chosen fabrics and cut out with a ¼-inch (6 mm) seam allowance around each piece. Next, trace the 12 flower petals and six leaves on the wrong side of your chosen fabrics and cut out on the drawn line.

2 Cut a square of background fabric 8½ x 8½ inches (21.6 x 21.6 cm). Using a light box or a bright window and the silver marking pencil, trace the cup, cup handle, and the inside of the cup on the fabric.

3 With matching cotton sewing thread and an appliqué needle, appliqué the inside of the teacup piece in place. Needle-turn appliqué is always worked from

right to left. Bring your needle up from the back of the block at the corner of the pattern drawn on your blue fabric. Use your needle to gently sweep a small section of the seam allowance under along the drawn line. Insert the needle straight down into the background fabric right next to the fold of your blue fabric. Taking a small stitch, bring the needle back to the front on the fold once again, catching a few threads of the blue fabric. You don't need to appliqué the bottom of the pattern because that will be covered when you appliqué the teacup in place.

4 Align the cup handle and pin in place. Appliqué the cup handle in place. To appliqué the inside curve of the handle, you'll need to clip an upside down Y-shape in the center of the seam allowance. Needle-turn appliqué the inside curve as before, using very tiny stitches and sweeping the seam allowance under with your needle. You don't need to appliqué the ends of the handle as they will be covered when you appliqué the teacup in place.

5 Position the teacup and pin in place. Appliqué the teacup in place as you did the cup inside and handle.

6 Position the leaves in place and pin. Embroider them to the background with an embroidery needle and yellow perle cotton, using a buttonhole embroidery stitch.

7 Position the flower petals and pin. Using the embroidery needle and the red perle cotton, attach the flower petals with a straight stitch similar to appliqué but working farther into the petal fabric.

8 To sew the flower stems, cut a piece of light emerald green silk ribbon embroidery ribbon 4 or 5 inches (10.2 or 12.7 cm) long for each stem. Using a chenille needle, take one long straight stitch starting at the lip of the cup and ending in the center of the flower.

9 Cut a 10 x 10-inch (25.4 x 25.4 cm) square of backing fabric and cotton batting. Layer the backing, batting, and quilt top and baste all three layers with cotton thread and a quilt-basting needle.

10 Using three strands of variegated embroidery floss and an embroidery needle, embroider the entire background of the quilt all the way to the edges of the quilt top with X's. The stitches should be randomly placed and vary slightly in size. Remove the basting stitches. Trim the excess batting and backing from the quilt so that it measures 8⅜ inches (21.3 cm) square.

11 Cut a straight strip of binding 2 inches x 44 inches (5.1 x 111.8 cm) from the binding fabric. Lay the strip horizontally with the wrong side facing up. Working with the left end of the strip, make a triangle fold, bringing the lower left corner up to meet the top raw edge of the strip and press. Clip excess fabric in the fold so that it's a generous ¼-inch (6 mm) seam allowance. Refold, and press the entire strip in half lengthwise.

12 Pin the binding in place, matching raw edges. Begin stitching about ½ inch (1.3 cm) below the angled fold and stop ¼ inch (6 mm) from the bottom edge of the quilt, using a ¼-inch (6 mm) seam allowance. Back tack at the beginning and the end of the stitching.

13 To form the mitered corner, first remove the quilt from the machine. Fold the binding strip at a 90-degree angle so that the raw edge of the binding and the raw edge of the next side of the quilt form a straight line. Fold the binding back along the quilt, matching raw edges, and pin. Begin stitching ¼ inch (6 mm) from the top and stop ¼ inch (6 mm) from the bottom. Back tack at the beginning and the end of the stitching. Work each corner in this manner. When you begin the last side, trim the excess binding at an angle so that it will gently slide inside the angled fold at the beginning of the binding. Pin in place, and beginning ¼ inch (6 mm) from the top edge, stitch this last side, stitching about 1 inch (2.5 cm) past the joint in the binding. Back tack the beginning and the end of the stitching.

14 Beading the quilt is done before you turn the binding with white beading thread and a beading needle. Beginning with the flower stems and using the chartreuse bugle beads, position the ribbon into the curve you want for the stem. While holding it in place, bring the beading needle up from the back of the quilt. Add one green bugle bead. With the bead laying flat against the ribbon, insert the needle back into the ribbon at the very end of the bead. Leave a small space and come up again, adding another bead and repeating the stitch.

15 To bead the flower centers, bring the needle up in the center of the flower. Add one large sequin, one medium square sequin, one round sequin and one cranberry seed bead. Skipping the cranberry bead, return needle back through all three sequins and back into the quilt. Go through each sequin and bead again, returning in the same manner and skipping the cranberry bead. This will secure the sequins and make the bead stand up with the side of the bead facing out.

16 Sew three sizes of clear rainbow sequins randomly over the surface of the teacup. Bring the needle up from the back and add a sequin followed by one cranberry seed bead. Skipping the seed bead as before, insert the needle back through the sequin. Repeat, skipping the seed bead again to secure the sequin.

17 Outline the entire teacup and handle with purple charlotte beads, using beading thread and the beading needle. Add five beads at a time, inserting the needle back into the quilt at the end of the line of beads and back up between beads 2 and 3 and through beads 3, 4, and 5 again. This keeps the beads close to the fabric and makes the next beads added fit snugly up against the first set with no gaps.

18 Outline the quilt with the brown bugle beads sewn right next to the binding.

19 Turn the quilt binding to the back and tack down with an appliqué stitch, using matching cotton thread and the appliqué needle. When you are finished turning the binding, stitch the fold where you joined the two ends of the binding closed.

spinning in orbit

*T*hink globally as you assemble this composition of rectangles, squares, and circles.

WHAT YOU NEED

Basic Quilting Tool Kit (page 11)

Template (page 138)

½ yard (45.7 cm) each of 8 different cotton fabrics

Template plastic

Permanent marker

Batting, 36 x 31 inches (.9 x .8 m)

Backing fabric, 36 x 31 inches (.9 x .8 m)

Needles for hand sewing and hand quilting

Cream embroidery floss

10 inches (25.4 cm) of 44-inch (1.1 m) wide fabric for binding

SEAM ALLOWANCE

¼ inch (6 mm), unless otherwise noted

FINISHED SIZE

33½ x 28½ inches (85 x 72.4 cm)

DESIGNER

KATE HENDERSON

WHAT YOU DO

1 Cut your eight fabrics to pieces in the following sizes:

- **Fabric A:** one 8½ inches (21.6 cm) x 28½ inches (72.5 cm) and one 6½ inches (16.5 cm) square

- **Fabric B:** one 10½ inches (26.7 cm) x 10 inches (25.4 cm) and one 5½ inches (14 cm) square

- **Fabric C:** one 10½ inches (26.7 cm) x 10 inches (24.5 cm) and one 5½ inches (14 cm) square

- **Fabric D:** one 10½ inches (26.7 cm) x 10 inches (24.5 cm)

- **Fabric E:** one 7½ inches (19 cm) x 28½ inches (72.5 cm) and one 4½ inches (11.4 cm) square

- **Fabric F:** 8½ inches (21.6 cm) x 17½ inches (44.5 cm) and one 4½ inches (11.4 cm) square

- **Fabric G:** one 4½ inches (11.4 cm) x 11½ inches (29.2 cm)

- **Fabric H:** one 4½ inches (11.4 cm) x 11½ inches

(29.2 cm) and one 6½ inches (16.5 cm) square

2 Following the photo with labels on page 113, sew as follows, ironing each seam as you go:

- Sew B to C and C to D along the 10½-inch (26.7 cm) edge.

- Sew G to H along the 11½-inch (29.2 cm) edge and then to F along the 8½-inch (21.6 cm) edge.

- Sew A to the B-C-D strip sewn above. Sew the other edge of B-C-D to E.

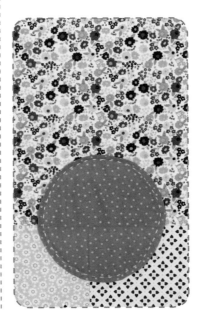

- Finally, sew E to the F-G-H strip sewn above.

3 Copy the template on page 138 and use the template plastic and a permanent marker to make three circle templates. You'll use these to cut circles from the square pieces of cut cloth. To do this, center the appropriate template over the right side of the fabric and trace around the circle with a fabric marker. Cut ¼ inch (6 mm) outside of the traced line. Match circle templates to squares as follows:

- Use the 3½-inch (8.9 cm) template for the 4½-inch (11.4 cm) squares of E and F.

- Use the 4½-inch (11.4 cm) template for 5½-inch (14 cm) squares of B and C.

- Use the 5½-inch (14 cm) template for the 6½-inch (16.5 cm) squares of A and H.

4 Press along the traced lines with your finger and pin the circles to the background, referring to the finished quilt picture for placement. Using thread to match the circle, slipstitch the circles to the background, tucking under the

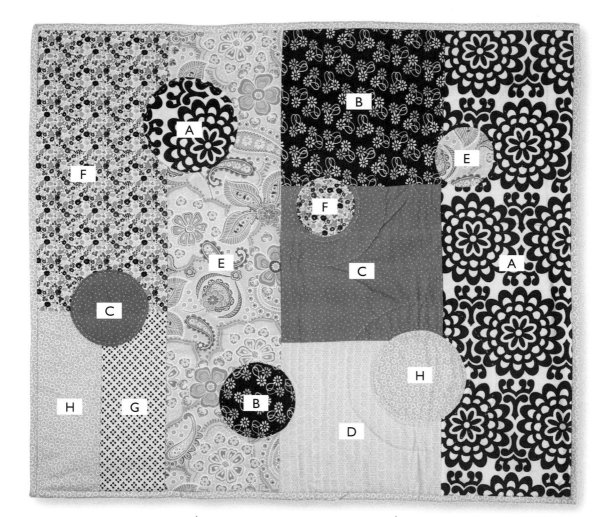

seam allowance with your needle as you go. Spray the circles with water to remove the marker.

5 Layer the quilt top, batting, and backing. Baste with safety pins or big running stitches.

6 Using two strands of cream embroidery floss and a needle, quilt ¼ inch (6 mm) inside the circles and then ¼ inch (6 mm) outside the circles and 1¾ inches (4.4 cm) outside the circles. Remove the safety pins.

7 Cut the binding fabric into four strips, each 2½ inches (6.4 cm) wide. Join and press the seams open. Press the strip in half along the length. Trim the backing and the batting and bind the quilt, mitering the corners.

give me a hand

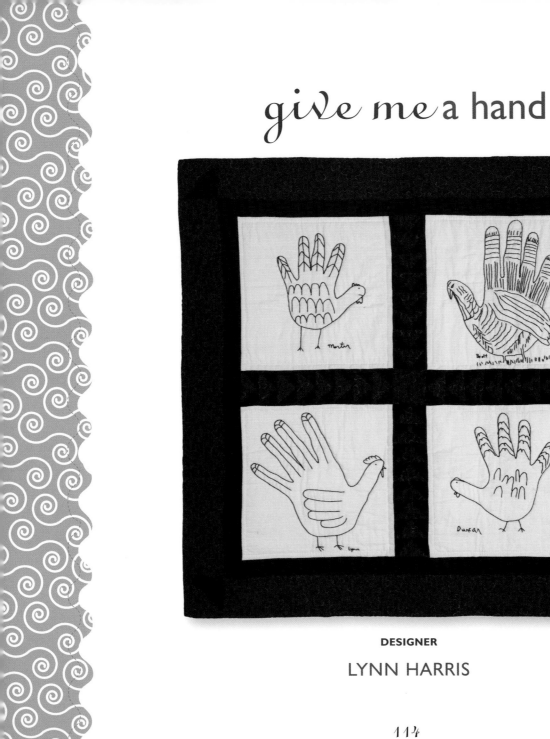

DESIGNER

LYNN HARRIS

WHAT YOU NEED

Basic Quilting Tool Kit (page 11)

Note: All fabric is 44 inches (1.1 m) wide.

Fine-point marking pen

½ yard (45.7 cm) muslin or other fabric for embroidery

Freezer paper

Red embroidery floss

Embroidery hoop

1 yard (.9 m) red print fabric

½ yard (45.7 cm) black fabric

1 yard (.9 m) backing fabric

1 yard (.9 m) square cotton batting

Hand-quilting thread and needle

SEAM ALLOWANCE

¼ inch (6 mm)

FINISHED SIZE

24 inches (61 cm) square

This family memory quilt was made with four squares for four family members. Feel free to adjust the size of the quilt to the size of your family.

WHAT YOU DO

1 Trace each family member's hand on a 9-inch (22.9 cm) square of paper. Have each person turn his or her hand tracing into a turkey. Everyone can be as creative as they like, but remember that the design will have to be embroidered and that the finished block size will be 8 inches (20.3 cm). Trace over the drawings with a dark fine-point marking pen

2 Cut a 12-inch (30.5 cm) square of muslin and a 12-inch (30.5 cm) square of freezer paper for each hand drawing. Press the shiny side of the freezer paper to the muslin to stabilize the fabric.

3 Use a light box or window to trace the designs on the fabric with a sharp pencil. Remove the freezer paper. Embroider each design with two strands of red embroidery floss, using an outline or stem stitch. Trim each square to 8½ inches (21.6 cm).

4 To make the "flying geese" sashing, first cut 32 1½ x 2 ½-inch (3.8 x 6.4 cm) rectangles for the geese from the red fabric. Cut two 3 inch (7.6 cm) squares from the red fabric for the cornerstones, and a 2½-inch (6.4 cm) square for the quilt center. Cut the cornerstone squares in half diagonally.

figure 1

figure 2

5 From the black fabric, cut 64 1½ x 1½-inch (3.8 x 3.8 cm) squares for the sky of the geese blocks and two 3-inch (7.6 cm) squares for the cornerstones. Cut the cornerstone squares in half diagonally.

6 Sew a sky piece to each geese rectangle as shown (figure 1). Press open. Repeat for the opposite side (figure 2). Press open. Trim the seams to ¼ inch (6 mm).

7 Sew the geese units together in groups of eight. Press.

8 Arrange the blocks and sashing. The quilt shown has all the geese in the sashing flying to the center of the quilt. Sew together. Press.

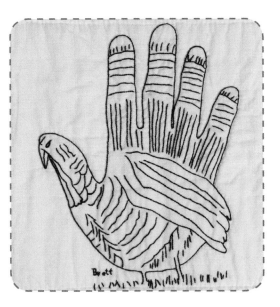

146

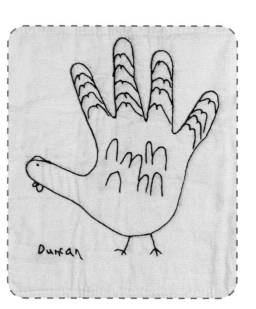

9 Measure the width of the quilt at this stage, then cut two 1½-inch (3.8 cm) wide border strips of black fabric and sew them to the sides of the quilt. Measure the quilt again side to side, then cut two 1½-inch (3.8 cm) strips of black fabric and sew them to the top and bottom of the quilt.

10 Cut four 2½-inch (6.4 cm) border strips of red fabric for the measured dimensions of the quilt.

11 Sew the four black cornerstone triangles to the four red cornerstone triangles to make four half-square triangles. Trim to 2½ inches (6.4 cm).

12 Lay out the quilt with the red border strips and cornerstones as shown in the photo. Sew together. Press well.

13 Layer the quilt top with the batting and backing. Baste. Hand quilt as desired. Quilt around each of the embroidered designs.

14 Trim the batting and the backing to the measured dimensions and bind the quilt.

THAT'S RIGHT! (OR LEFT)

For variety, you'll probably want to trace some right and some left hands so that the turkeys don't all face the same way.

the elusive batiki bird

You say you've never even heard of a batiki bird before? Now that you've spotted one, it's time to make your own.

DESIGNER

SARAH ANN SMITH

WHAT YOU NEED

Basic Quilting Tool Kit (page 11)

4 pieces of white-on-white print, each 7 x 30 inches (17.8 x 76.2 cm)

1 piece of pale green-gray fabric, 5 x 30 inches (12.7 x 76.2 cm)

14 to 16 pieces of blue, teal, and green batiks, 2½ to 4 inches (6.4 to 10.2 cm) wide by 7 inches (17.8 cm) long

Fusible web, 9 x 12 inches (22.9 x 30.5 cm)

Hot pink/orange batik, 9 x 12 inches (22.9 x 30.5 cm)

Variegated embroidery floss in magenta/pink and orange/yellow

Embroidery needle and hoop

Cotton fabric for backing, 30 inches (76.2 cm) square

Cotton batting, 29 inches (73.6 cm) square

Quilting thread in complementary colors

½ yard (45.7 cm) batik or near solid for binding

SEAM ALLOWANCE

¼ inch (6 mm)

FINISHED SIZE

26½ inches (67.3 cm) square

WHAT YOU DO

CUTTING AND PIECING

1 To make the background, cut each white-on-white fabric into four long wedges; one wedge should be about 3½ inches (8.9 cm) on the wide end. Cut the remaining section into three pieces with the narrowest end no smaller than 1 inch (2.5 cm) wide.

2 Cut the pale green-gray fabric into three long wedges with the narrow end no narrower than about 1 inch (2.5 cm).

3 Lay out your strips, alternating fabrics. Turn so that approximately every other one the wide end of the wedge is at the top. Using a washable marking pen or pencil, number your strips at the very bottom from left to right so the order doesn't get confused while stitching.

4 Machine-piece six to eight strips to make the section to the left of the tree trunk about 8 to 9 inches (20.3 to 22.9 cm) wide. Machine-piece the remaining strips for the section to the right of the tree trunk. Press all seam allowances toward the tree trunk.

5 To make the tree trunk and branches, cut each small chunk of the blues, teals, and greens into two wedges. As you did with the background, alternate the wide end of the strips to create a stack of "logs" 30 to 32 inches (76.2 to 81.3 cm) long. Trim the edges and cut your tree trunk to be 3½ inches (8.9 cm) wide at the bottom and 2½ inches (6.4 cm) wide at the top.

6 Cut the remaining piece of fabric into two narrower strips, at least 1 inch (2.5 cm) wide on the narrow end, to use for the branches. Press all seam allowances in one direction.

INSTANT VARIETY

If you don't have an extensive stash, look for some fat quarters that have a lot of color variation in them, then "swiss cheese" cut chunks from various parts of the fat quarter to make it look like they were cut from different fabrics.

7 To piece the background to the tree, place your tree trunk so that it overlaps the two background pieces. Cut the background pieces along the edges of the tree trunk. Place the remaining two narrower strips of tree as branches. Divide the long strip on the left and use the remainder for the small upper branch on the right.

8 Using a washable marking pencil or pen, mark the outside edge of your branches. Remove the branch, then mark ½ inch (1.3 cm) inside this line. These inner (pink) lines will be your cutting lines (and not the outside line).

9 Piece your background as shown in the photo in this order. Sew the left branch to the upper and lower background pieces. Sew the small upper branch on the right to the small triangle of background and the center background section. Sew the larger branch on the right to the upper and lower portions of the background. Press the seams toward the branches so that the branches appear to be in front of the background.

CREATING THE APPLIQUÉ BIRD

10 Apply fusible web to the back of your bird fabric. Mark the outline of the bird (by copying the bird here or creating your own) and cut out. Position your bird using the quilt photo as a guide and fuse in place.

11 You can embroider the bird now or after you have quilted this piece. If you wait until later, the back of your embroidery stitches will show on the back of your quilt. You can embroider as you wish: The quilt pictured here uses strands of pink variegated and yellow-orange floss in different combinations, with a feather stitch for outlining and a straight stitch elsewhere. Whether you embroider before or after quilting, a hoop will keep the top flat as you stitch.

12 When the top is done, press and trim to 28 x 28 inches (71.1 x 71.1 cm). Make sure the overall impression of the background piecing and tree trunk is vertical, not tilted.

A PAINTER'S LIGHT

You can create a subtle sense of space by selecting light and dark shades of the same color for your quilting and arranging them to make it appear the light is coming from one direction. For example, the tree trunk here uses a medium-dark blue on the left side for the contour lines, and a brighter aqua on the right side, the side of the light source.

LAYERING AND QUILTING

13 Place your backing fabric face up on the table, then the batting, and finally your neatly pressed top. Baste using your favorite method.

14 Hand- or machine-quilt the piece. First, quilt in the ditch (on the background side of the piecing lines, right next to the seam line) around the tree trunk and branches.

15 When the quilting is complete, square up your quilt to 26½ inches (67.3 cm) square.

BINDING

16 Use the method of binding you prefer. This quilt was made with a bias-double-fold binding for strength and sturdiness. To make this binding, first cut bias strips 3½ inches (8.9 cm) wide. You will need about 110 running inches (2.8 m) of bias.

17 Sew the strips together and press the seams open. Fold the bias in half and sew to your quilt, finishing the ends and sewing down using the technique you like best.

attic treasures

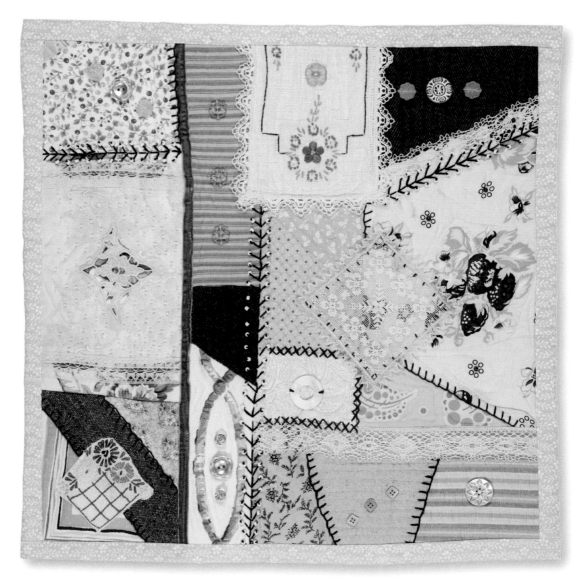

*W*herever the materials for this quilt come from—old tablecloths, worn-out clothing, a vintage store—use them to create a story of time gone by. It's history in the making.

WHAT YOU NEED

Basic Quilting Tool Kit (page 11)

18-inch (45.7 cm) square piece of scrap paper

Scraps of your favorite fabrics (cotton prints, wool, flannel)

White sewing thread

Quilt batting, 18 inches (45.7 cm) square

Muslin fabric, 19 inches (48.3 cm) square

Invisible thread

Scraps of old linens (embroidered or printed)

Assorted lace pieces and ribbons

18 inches (45.7 cm) of ⅜-inch (9.5 mm) wide green velvet ribbon

Embroidery needle (with a large enough eye for embroidery floss, but small enough to pass through size E beads)

Red and black embroidery floss

100 white beads, size E

Beading needle

100 pearl seed beads

15 red glass beads, size E

Assorted buttons

Red ticking fabric, 18 inches (45.7 cm) square

½ yard (45.7 cm) cotton print fabric for the edge

SEAM ALLOWANCE

¼ inch (6 mm)

FINISHED SIZE

19 x 18½ inches (48.3 x 47 cm)

DESIGNER

JOAN K. MORRIS

WHAT YOU DO

1 Use the 18-inch (45.7 cm) square of scrap paper as a guide for laying out your scraps of fabric. Play around with placement, size, shape, and color. You want to combine several small pieces into larger rows or blocks of fabric for easier joining later (figure 1).

figure 1

2 With the white thread, sew your pieces together in rows and blocks. Press all seams open. Don't worry if the blocks aren't perfectly square or rectangular. Join all the rows and blocks into a large square. Don't worry about the size, as you will cut it down to an 18-inch (45.7 cm) square later.

3 Center the square of batting under the sewn quilt top. Center the square of muslin under the batting. Pin all three layers in place.

4 Using invisible thread in the top of the machine and white thread in the bobbin, stitch from the top on each seam line ("stitch in the ditch") and around the whole edge of the piece. Start in the center and work your way to the edge to keep the muslin flat underneath.

5 Begin quilting each section of fabric by following the design pattern on the fabric, stitching around shapes, or following stripes or checks. Make each section different, with stitching rows anywhere from ¼ inch to ¾ inch (6 mm to 1.9 cm) apart.

6 Stitch on the lace and ribbon pieces with a straight stitch along all edges. Stitch on any cut-out embroidered pieces using a small zigzag stitch around the whole edge to stop any fraying.

7 Use the embroidery needle and floss to stitch on the blanket stitch, the "x" stitch, and the beaded stitch (using the white beads) along some of the seam lines, and also to embellish the lace with a small stitch.

8 Use the beading needle and white thread to attach the small pearl seed beads. Use the invisible thread to attach the red size E beads and the buttons. When

placing the beads and buttons, be sure to keep them 1 inch (2.5 cm) in from the edge so you can sew on the backing and edge pieces without breaking your machine needle on the beads.

9 Once you have placed all the embellishments, center the square of red ticking fabric on the back of the quilt, right side out, and pin in place.

10 Machine-stitch all the way around the edge, ½ inch (1.3 cm) in from the edge of the red ticking fabric. Trim the quilted piece to match the red ticking fabric backing all the way around the edge.

TURN, TURN, TURN

To quilt the pieces together for the top, you'll have to do a lot of lifting of the presser foot and turning of the piece. Just roll up the excess so it fits in the sewing machine.

11 Cut two pieces of the cotton edge fabric, each 5 x 18 inches (12.7 x 45.7 cm), and two more, each 5 x 20 inches (12.7 x 50.8 cm).

12 Along one of the side edges of the quilt, place one of the 5 x 18-inch (12.7 x 45.7 cm) pieces right sides together with the quilt and stitch ½ inch (1.3 cm) in from the edge. Press the piece to the back of the quilt, creating a ½-inch (1.3 cm) edge on the front. Fold the edge piece in half to the inside and press flat, creating a 2-inch (5.1 cm) back edge. Pin in place. Repeat along the other side edge.

13 For the bottom edge, center one of the 5 x 20-inch (12.7 x 50.8 cm) pieces right sides together and stitch ½ inch (1.3 cm) in from the edge.

Fold the sides in first to cover the side edges and then fold the whole thing to the back and press. Fold the edge piece in half to the inside and press and pin in place.

14 On the top edge, to create a pocket for hanging the piece, center the other 5 x 20-inch (12.7 x 50.8 cm) edge piece right sides together and stitch ½ inch (1.3 cm) in from the edge. Fold and press the sides in, and then the long edge in half to the inside, but this time machine-stitch the side edge in place so there is only one hole for the pocket. Pin in place.

15 With white thread, hand-stitch the whole edge piece to the back, leaving the top side edge open for the pocket.

star & cross

Two for the price of one: On this small scale, two traditional patterns make for a perfect distillation of the quilter's art of combining squares and triangles.

DESIGNER

LYNDA RAPP

WHAT YOU NEED

Basic Quilting Tool Kit (page 11)

Templates (page 139)

Tissue paper or foundation paper for pattern

Fabric for each block: 3 fat quarters, 2 in contrasting colors such as blue and red or blue and yellow and 1 in a background color such as white

Low-loft batting, 2 5-inch (12.7 cm) squares

Backing fabric, 2 5-inch (12.7 cm) squares

Hand-quilting needles

Contrasting quilting thread

SEAM ALLOWANCE

¼ inch (6 mm)

FINISHED SIZE

Ohio Star: 4½ inches (11.4 cm) square; Odd Fellow's Cross: 4¼ inches (10.8 cm) square

WHAT YOU DO

 Before you begin, a few helpful hints for paper-piecing these blocks:

- The paper side is the wrong side of the block.

- The unmarked side of the paper is the fabric side.

- The marked side of the paper is the top for stitching.

- To avoid confusion, it helps to label the paper with your fabric colors.

- Set your sewing machine stitch length to 18 to 20 stitches per inch (2.5 cm), and use a 90/14 sewing machine needle, as it perforates the paper, making it easier to tear the paper away later.

- After each piece is placed and sewn, trim the excess seam allowance to ¼ inch (6 mm) or less as it makes the block less bulky for hand quilting later.

- Always add fabric pieces in number order and sew on each line at least ¼ inch (6 mm) beyond the marked lines.

MAKING THE OHIO STAR QUILT

2 From the blue fabric, cut straight-grain binding strips 1½ inches (3.8 cm) wide and long enough to go around the quilt with enough extra length to join. Set aside. Cut one 2½-inch (6.4 cm) square.

3 From the red fabric, cut a 2-inch (5.1 cm) strip. From this strip cut four 2-inch (5.1 cm) squares. Then cut them across the diagonal to make eight half-square triangles.

4 From the white background fabric, cut a 2½-inch (6.4 cm) strip. From this strip cut six 2½-inch (6.4 cm) squares. Cut two of those squares across the diagonal to make four half-square triangles. You should have four squares and four triangles.

5 Copy the pattern on page 139 by enlarging it onto tissue or foundation paper.

6 To begin assembly: Place the white fabric for piece #1

right side up on the unmarked side of the paper and pin in. Always make sure that the fabric covers the marked area with at least ¼ inch (6 mm) extra for seam allowance.

7 Place red triangle piece #2 right sides together on top of piece #1 and pin on the paper side. Trim any excess seam allowance. Press open.

8 Place red triangle piece #3 right side together on top of piece #1, pin and stitch on the line between piece 1 and 3. Trim and press.

9 In the same manner, continue across the row for pieces 4 and 5, trimming and pressing as you sew each piece. Set row 1 aside.

10 Row 2 is done in two parts and then sewn together. First paper-piece section 1, then paper-piece section 2 as above. With the fabric side down on the cutting mat, use a rotary cutter and ruler to trim the edges to a 1¼-inch (6 mm) seam allowance. Sew these two sections together to complete the row. Press toward the blue piece.

11 Sew row 3 as you did row 1. With the fabric side down on a cutting mat, use the rotary cutter and ruler to trim the edges of sections to the ¼-inch (6 mm) seam allowance.

12 Sew row 1 to row 2 matching the seams. Sew row 3 to row 2. Press.

13 Square up the block with the rotary cutter and ruler, leaving a ¼-inch (6 mm) seam allowance. Remove the paper.

14 Sandwich the block with thin batting and backing. Pin or baste together. Sew on binding using a ¼-inch (6 mm) seam allowance; miter the corners. Fold under the raw edges, pin, and blind stitch. Quilt as desired.

LOOK TO THE LIGHT

Because you are working with the fabric under the paper, you can hold your project up to a light source to help visualize that the fabric is properly placed to include enough for the block plus the seam allowances.

MAKING THE
ODD FELLOW'S CROSS

15 From the blue fabric, cut straight-grain binding strips 1½ inches (3.8 cm) wide and long enough to go around the quilt with enough to join. Set aside. Cut a 1¾-inch (4.4 cm) strip. From this strip cut six 1¾-inch (4.4 cm) squares. Cut those squares in half diagonally to make 12 half-square triangles.

16 From the white background fabric, cut a 2½-inch (6.4 cm) strip. From this strip cut two 2½-inch (6.4 cm) squares. Cut those in half diagonally to make four half-square triangles. Cut a 1¾-inch (4.4 cm) strip. From this strip cut 14 1¾-inch (4.4 cm) squares. Cut those in half diagonally to make 28 half-square triangles.

17 From the yellow fabric, cut one 2-inch (5.1 cm) square.

18 Copy the pattern on page 139 by enlarging it onto tissue or foundation paper.

19 For row 1, place the smaller white triangle for piece #1 right side up on the unmarked side of the paper and pin in place. Always make sure that the fabric covers the marked area with at least ¼ inch (6 mm) extra for seam allowance.

20 Place blue triangle piece #2 right sides together on top of piece #1 and pin on the paper side. Trim excess seam allowance. Press open.

21 Place white piece #3 on top of piece #2 right sides together, pin and sew on line between piece 2 and 3. Trim and press.

22 Continue in the same manner in number order, trimming and pressing after each piece. Set row 1 aside.

23 Row 2 is done in three parts and then sewn together to complete the row. First paper-piece section 1 and section 3 in the same manner as row 1. With the fabric side down on a cutting mat, use a rotary cutter and ruler to trim the edges of section 1 and section 3 to a ¼-inch (6 mm) seam allowance.

24 Join section 1 to 2 and press toward the yellow, then sew section 3 to that piece. Press toward the yellow.

25 Sew row 3 as you did row 1. With the fabric side down on the cutting mat, use the rotary cutter and ruler to trim the edges to a ¼-inch (6 mm) seam allowance.

26 Sew row 1 to row 2 matching seams, then sew row 3 to row 2. Press.

27 Square up with the rotary cutter and ruler, leaving a 1¼-inch (6 mm) seam allowance. Remove the paper.

28 Sandwich the block with thin batting and backing. Pin or baste together. Sew on the binding using the marked ¼-inch (6 mm) seam allowance; miter the corners. Fold under the raw edges, pin, and blind stitch. Quilt as desired.

shrine to pretty little things

If you're reading this book, you must like things that are pretty and little. Now it's time to show how much you really care.

DESIGNER

JAMIE FINGAL

WHAT YOU NEED

Basic Quilting Tool Kit (page 11)

1 yard (.9 m) fabric for background

1½ yards (1.4 m) fabric for border and backing

¼ yard (22.9 cm) fabric with a wood print

¼ yard (22.9 cm) black fabric for outline of shrine

¼ yard (22.9 cm) fabric for background in shrine

Fusible web

Graph paper

Parchment paper

1 yard (.9 m) wool felt or a blend of rayon and wool

Embellishments, such as a zipper, mini safety pins, a mini belt buckle, a cloth measuring tape, silver snaps and buttons, mini pearl beads, a doll purse and shoes, a crown charm, and lace

Black embroidery thread

Waxed bead thread

Embroidery needle

Small needle for beading

Fabric glue

SEAM ALLOWANCE

None

FINISHED SIZE

16¼ x 21½ inches
(41.3 x 54.6 cm)

WHAT YOU DO

1 Choose contrasting fabrics for the interior of the shrine and the background. You want the colors to pop when they are together.

2 Iron all your fabrics onto the fusible web. Draw your design for the shrine on graph paper.

3 Start building your shrine. Lay the pattern onto the wood fabric and pin it into place. Cut it out along the outer edge.

4 Lay the wood-fabric shrine onto parchment paper (to protect your iron) and iron into place. Cut ¼-inch (6 mm) strips of the black fabric to use as an outline for the shrine. Lift up the outer edges of the shrine carefully and lay the strips underneath, ironing them into place as you go. Continue all the way around.

5 Cut the three pieces of fabric for the interior of the shrine as follows: a triangle with a base 5½ inches (14 cm) wide and sides measuring 3⅞ inches (9.8 cm) each for the roof; a rectangle, 4¾ x 5½ inches (12 x 14 cm) for the middle; and a rectangular strip for the lower section, 6¾ x 2¼ inches (17.1 x 5.7 cm). Center the pieces on the appropriate parts of the shrine, making sure the middle section is about 1 inch (2.5 cm) from the shrine sides. Iron into place.

6 With the ¼-inch (6 mm) strips that you have left over, outline the triangle top interior section and the bottom section. Use two strips to divide the latter into three square openings.

7 Lay the background fabric (the blue fabric in the photo) on top of the felt, making sure that it reaches about 1 to 2 inches (2.5 to 5.1 cm) from the edges of the felt. Iron it down so that it is flat and smooth.

8 Remove the shrine from the parchment paper and place it on top of the background fabric.

Center it into place and iron it down.

9 Pin down the measuring tape around the center interior section of the shrine, leaving about ½ inch (1.3 cm) of wood fabric on the sides. Take apart the zipper and cut it to fit into place, under the inside portion of the measuring tape, and re-pin it. With a zipper foot on your sewing machine, sew the zipper into place along the inside edge of the measuring tape. Then, with your regular foot and black thread, sew the zigzag stitch on the outer edges of the measuring tape.

10 Cut out the dress, and iron it on in the middle of the middle interior rectangle. Then sew it into place using a free-motion foot.

11 Sew the entire shrine onto the background with black thread, using the zigzag stitch with a free-motion foot. Then change the stitch to straight, and free-motion the wood patterns in the shrine fabric to add texture to your piece.

12 Change the thread to match the background, and free-motion machine-quilt it down.

13 Cut four pieces of fabric, each about 5 inches (12.7 cm) wide, for the border. Make the curved edge by trimming the fabric strips on one side, cutting around the flowers in the fabric pattern.

14 Place the border fabric on each side so it extends about 2 to 3½ inches (5.1 to 8.9 cm) into the center. The remainder of the border strip will wrap around the edge of the quilt to the back. Begin ironing down the border one side at a time, flipping the quilt over to iron the fabric to the back. Clip excess fabric in the corners if needed. You will secure this into place later.

15 Begin attaching the embellishments. For the mini pearls on the dress, hand sew using a beading needle and waxed bead thread. Sew the pearls on one at a time with a double thread, knotting it on the back of the piece.

16 Sew the buttons on one of the three openings in the bottom section of the shrine, using perle cotton thread, going through each hole twice and knotting on the back to secure. Hand sew on the lace in the middle portion. You can glue smaller embellishments into place with the adhesive, applying it with a toothpick and letting it dry 24 hours, before you go back and sew them into place. Sew the medium silver snaps onto the four corners of the center section of the shrine.

17 Glue and sew the doll accessories into place on the top portion, along with the crown. Using one of your tiny buttons, sew black thread through it twice and knot it, then place it with a drop of glue onto the purse.

18 Using the black embroidery thread, sew a running stitch just inside the interior pieces of fabric on the shrine.

19 For the backing, place your quilt face down on an ironing surface. Cut the backing to cover the felt, which should be about ¾ to 1 inch (1.9 to 2.5 cm) from the sides. Iron it on carefully, so as not to disturb the embellishments on the front.

20 With black thread in your machine, sew around the outer portion of the shrine. Then change your thread to match the border fabric color and free-motion machine-quilt the entire border.

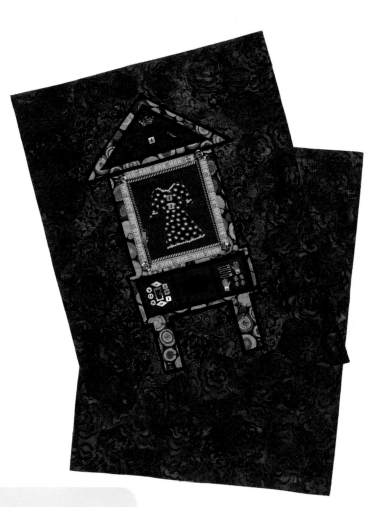

FUSE OR LOSE

Fusible web is truly one of the sewing world's great inventions. In this project, the entire piece has been fused to black wool felt. Each section was fused individually and the backing was fused on as well.

through the labyrinth

DESIGNER

LISA M. PENNY

$\mathcal{G}$arden labyrinths are intended to be restful and meditative, and this quilt is just that, both for the viewer and the maker.

WHAT YOU NEED

Basic Quilting Tool Kit (page 11)

Note: All fabrics and fusible interfacing are 42 inches (106.7 cm) wide.

1¼ yards (1.13 m) fusible quilter's grid

½ yard (45.7 cm) white with lavender fabric

¾ yard (68.6 cm) light green print fabric

¼ yard (22.9 cm) of evergreen fabric

Mini iron (optional)

½ yard (45.7 cm) of lime green fabric

1 yard (.9 m) print fabric for backing

Cotton/polyester fusible batting

Optional embellishments: seed, glass, and lampworked beads; silk ribbon; and satin roses

SEAM ALLOWANCE

¼ inch (6 mm)

FINISHED SIZE

32 inches (81.3 cm) square

WHAT YOU DO

1 Cut a piece of fusible quilter's grid at 41 inches (104.14 cm) square, using the 1-inch grid measurement printed on it. This will leave a 1-inch (2.5 cm) margin around the fabric top.

2 Cut 266 squares from the white and lavender fabric, 311 squares from the green print fabric, and 99 squares from the evergreen fabric, with all squares 1½ inches (3.8 cm) each.

3 Starting from the top left corner of the fusible grid, count one block to the right and one block down. Place one evergreen fabric square on the

grid with the top and left sides of the fabric aligned with the grid lines. Lightly press the square into position using the mini iron, or the front tip of a full-sized iron. By pressing gently, the pieces can be removed and repositioned if necessary. It's best to wait until the top is fully positioned before ironing firmly.

4 Place a second evergreen fabric square to the right of the first, aligning the top and right edges of the fabric with the grid lines. Press gently into position. How the fabric squares fit on the grid will start to become clear: There are two fabric squares for every three grid squares. By aligning the outer edges of the fabric squares with the grid lines, all of the fabric squares will perfectly align.

5 Continue to place the fabric squares onto the grid, aligning the edges as in step 4, pressing gently with each placement, following the chart on page 137 for the placement of the colors. Note that the border is not placed on the grid, but is added after the center labyrinth is sewn.

6 After checking your place-ment to ensure the pathways are accurate, fuse all of the fabric squares permanently into position by pressing for approximately five to eight seconds. (Follow the di-rections for the fusible grid.) Press by placing your iron directly down in one corner, then lifting it and placing it directly down in sections. Do not run the iron side-to-side, as your fabric squares will shift and crease. This step is easier to do on a large flat surface on top of a large towel or folded sheet, rather than on a narrow ironing board. When the front has been pressed, flip it gently over and lightly press again from the back side.

7 Fold the first column so the right sides go together. The top will crease in a straight line, along the edge of the fabric squares. Sew a scant ¼-inch

(6 mm) seam down the length of the column. Then fold over the second column, and sew a scant ¼ inch (6 mm) along the fold line. The fold will fall along one of the grid lines on every other column. Repeat this for each of the 25 columns.

8 Press the top to flatten it, with all seams going in the same direction.

9 To avoid bulky seams when sewing the rows, place the top face down, and gently tear the grid interfacing between the fabric squares. The interfacing will easily tear down to the previously sewn seam, making it possible to flatten the seam allowances when folding each row together for sewing.

10 Repeating the process as in step 7, fold the first row, right sides together, and sew

a scant ¼ inch (6 mm) along the fold. Split the allowances from the column seams, to avoid bulk at the corners.

11 Press to flatten. It is easier to press first on the back, to flatten the seams, then on the front.

12 Cut the border strips from the lime green fabric: two strips at 3½ x 26½ inches (8.9 x 67.3 cm) and two strips at 3½ x 32½ inches (8.9 x 83.3 cm). Measure your fused and sewn labyrinth before cutting the borders, and adjust the length of the strips to accommodate any variance you may have had in your seam allowance.

13 Sew the short strips along the sides of the labyrinth, and sew the long strips along the top and bottom.

14 Cut the backing fabric 36 inches (91 cm) square. Cut the fusible batting 36 inches (91 cm) square.

15 Assemble the quilt sandwich as you would with traditional basting or pinning methods, but instead of pinning,

BIG AS LIFE

Here's a neat trick to try: Bring the chart for this project to your local copy shop, and have them enlarge it so that each square on the chart measures 1½ inches (3.8 cm). You may need to copy it in sections and tape them together. You can then place the full-size chart under your fusible grid. Since you can see through the lightweight grid, following the place-ment for the fabric squares will be easy.

simply press with a hot iron for about eight seconds, starting at the center and working outward to the edges. Then gently flip the quilt and press again from the back, easing out any tucks or folds from the center outward. If the sandwich loosens as you work on the quilting, simply press again to renew the hold.

16 Quilt the piece by "stitching-in-the-ditch," running a stitch line along all of the vertical column lines, then along all of the horizontal row lines. For additional decorative quilting, try using stippling along the white paths, either free-motion or with a pre-programmed stipple stitch.

17 Use the remaining light green fabric for the binding method of your choice.

18 You can add various embellishments if you wish. The quilt pictured includes colored glass and lampworked beads, seed beads in pastel colors, Swarovski crystal beads in the swirls of the border, a few satin roses, and silk yarn with knotted flowers.

E	E	E	E	E	E	E	E	E	E	E	E	E	E	E	E	E	E	E	E	E	E	E	E	E	E	E	E
E	LG	LG	LG	LG	LG	LG	LG	LG	LG	LG	LG	LG	LG	LG	LG	LG	LG	LG	LG	LG	LG	LG	LG	LG	LG	LG	E
E	LG	W	W	W	W	W	W	W	W	W	W	W	LG	W	W	W	W	W	W	W	W	W	W	W	W	LG	E
E	LG	W	LG	LG	LG	LG	LG	LG	LG	LG	LG	W	LG	W	LG	LG	LG	LG	LG	LG	LG	LG	LG	W	LG	E
E	LG	W	LG	W	W	W	W	W	W	W	W	W	LG	W	LG	W	W	W	W	W	W	W	W	LG	W	LG	E
E	LG	W	LG	W	LG	LG	LG	LG	LG	LG	LG	LG	LG	W	LG	LG	LG	LG	LG	LG	LG	LG	W	LG	W	LG	E
E	LG	W	LG	W	LG	W	W	W	W	W	W	W	LG	W	W	W	W	W	W	W	W	LG	W	LG	W	LG	E
E	LG	W	LG	W	LG	W	LG	LG	LG	LG	LG	W	LG	W	LG	LG	LG	LG	LG	LG	LG	W	LG	W	LG	E
E	LG	W	LG	W	LG	W	LG	W	W	W	W	W	LG	W	W	W	W	W	W	W	LG	W	LG	W	LG	E
E	LG	W	LG	W	LG	W	LG	W	LG	LG	LG	LG	LG	LG	LG	LG	W	LG	W	LG	W	LG	E
E	LG	W	LG	W	LG	W	LG	W	LG	W	W	W	W	W	W	W	LG	W	LG	W	LG	W	LG	E
E	LG	W	LG	W	LG	W	LG	W	W	W	LG	LG	LG	LG	W	W	LG	W	LG	W	LG	W	LG	E
E	LG	W	LG	LG	LG	LG	LG	LG	LG	LG	LG	W	W	LG	LG	LG	LG	LG	LG	LG	LG	W	LG	E
E	LG	W	W	W	W	W	W	W	W	W	W	W	LG	W	LG	LG	LG	LG	LG	W	LG	W	LG	E
E	LG	W	LG	W	LG	W	LG	W	W	W	W	W	LG	W	W	W	W	W	W	W	LG	W	LG	E
E	LG	W	LG	W	LG	W	LG	LG	LG	LG	W	LG	W	LG	LG	LG	LG	LG	W	LG	W	LG	E
E	LG	W	LG	W	LG	W	LG	W	W	W	W	LG	W	LG	LG	LG	W	LG	W	LG	W	LG	E
E	LG	W	LG	W	LG	W	LG	W	LG	LG	LG	LG	W	LG	W	LG	LG	LG	W	LG	W	LG	E
E	LG	W	LG	W	LG	W	W	W	W	W	W	W	LG	W	LG	W	W	W	W	W	LG	W	LG	E
E	LG	W	LG	LG	LG	LG	LG	LG	LG	LG	LG	LG	W	LG	LG	LG	LG	LG	LG	LG	W	LG	E
E	LG	W	LG	LG	LG	LG	LG	LG	LG	LG	LG	W	LG	LG	LG	LG	LG	LG	LG	LG	LG	W	LG	E
E	LG	W	W	W	W	W	W	W	W	W	W	W	LG	W	LG	W	W	W	W	W	W	W	LG	E
E	LG	LG	LG	LG	LG	LG	LG	LG	LG	LG	LG	LG	W	LG	LG	LG	LG	LG	LG	LG	LG	LG	LG	E
E	E	E	E	E	E	E	E	E	E	E	E	E	E	W	E	E	E	E	E	E	E	E	E	E	E	E	E

E = Evergreen (the outer wall of the labyrinth)
LG = Light Green (the garden hedges forming the walls)
W = White with lavender (the light pathways to follow to the center)

RELOCATING YOUR QUILT

Consider changing the theme of the labyrinth to an island paradise, using paths the color of beach sand and walls in tropical ocean batiks, or to a jungle picture with light grassy pathways and fabrics in deep jungle and animal prints.

templates

Whimsical Rose, page 83
(enlarge 200%)

3½
4½
5½

Spinning in Orbit, page 111
(enlarge 200%)

Star & Cross, page 126
(enlarge 200%)

Ohio Star

Odd Fellow's Cross

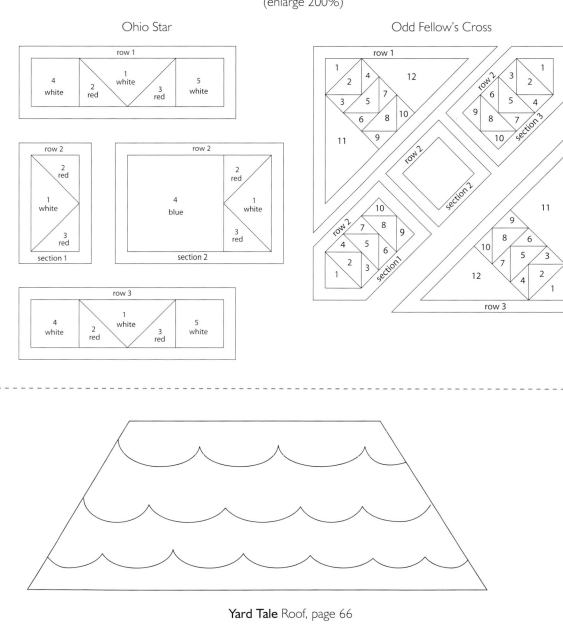

Yard Tale Roof, page 66
(enlarge 200%)

Vegetables, actual size

Door, actual size

Garden, enlarge 300%

Clothes, actual size

Tree, enlarge 300%

Square Deal, page 60
(enlarge 400%)

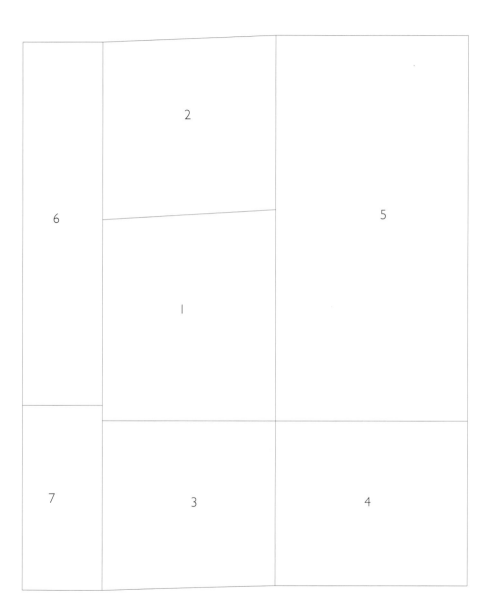

2

6

5

1

7

3

4

about the designers

ROXANNE BEAUVAIS has an online shop (www.feminineaddictions. etsy.com) that carries vintage fabric, unique finds, and one-of-a-kind designs. Visit her blog at www. craftaddictions.blogspot.com.

AMANDA CARESTIO is an editorial assistant with Lark Books by day and a serial crafter all other times. See more of her stitched distractions online at www.digsandbean.blogspot.com.

CINDY COOKSEY has had quilts published in the magazines *Quilters Newsletter* and *Quilts Japan* and in the books *Quilt Visions 2002*, *Portfolio 14 and 15*, and *Embellished Mini-Quilts* (Lark Books, 2007).
See more of her work at www.cindycooksey.com and www.cookseyville.blogspot.com.

JANET COOPER'S recent work collects the faded printed fabrics of unfinished quilts, embroidered tea towels, buttons, vintage evening gowns, and memorabilia into textile assemblages. See more of her creations at www. janetcooperdesigns.com.

KATHY DANIELS has shown her work at sidewalk art festivals, gift shops, and small gallery shows. She also writes and shares her works in progress at her blog www. studiointhewoods.blogspot.com.

MALKA DUBRAWSKY'S work has been included in a number of shows and in such publications as the *Quilt National* series, *Fiberarts Design Book 7*, *Quilts, Baby!* (Lark Books, 2009), and *Quilting Arts* magazine. See her quilts, pillows, and other sundries at her online store www.stitchindye.etsy.com.

JAMIE FINGAL is the author of *Embellished Mini-Quilts* (Lark Books, 2007), and she was a featured guest on the PBS show *Quilting Arts TV*. Learn about her work at www.jamiefingal.com and on her blog at www. jamiefingaldesigns.blogspot.com.

CHEYENNE GOH spends her time dreaming up new ways of recycling wearables and other things into objects of fun and function, like the Recycled Suits Bags and cozies she sells in her online store at www.rumahkampung. etsy.com.

LYNN HARRIS writes about her daily life and shares photographs of her creations on her blog at www.thelittleredhen.typepad.com.

KATE HENDERSON lives in the southwest of Western Australia with her husband and three girls. She sells her work under the name Two Little Banshees, named after her twins, at www. neverenoughhours.etsy.com, and she writes about crafting at www. neverenoughhours.blogspot.com.

ALYSSE HENNESSEY loves designing projects, hiking, and making cupcakes in weird colors. Visit her blog at www.blissmonkeystudio. blogspot.com and her online shop at www.alythered.etsy.com.

MARY HUBBARD lives in Maryland with her husband, two sons, and two daughters. See her work at www.whitecloverstitches.etsy. com as well as on www.flickr.com/ whitecloverstitches.

SHELECE JORGENSEN became intrigued by African story quilts, which led her to make her own quilts that capture all of life's little happy moments. She sells her little quilts at www.etsy.com/shop.php?user_id=45492.

REBEKA LAMBERT has contributed to other Lark Books, including *Pretty Little Potholders*, *Pretty Little Patchwork*, and *Pretty Little Purses & Pouches*. She has a blog at www.artsycraftybabe.typepad.com and an online shop at www.artsycraftybabe.etsy.com.

JOAN K. MORRIS has contributed projects to many publications from Lark Books, including *50 Nifty Beaded Cards*, *Extreme Office Crafts*, *Cutting-Edge Decoupage*, *Pretty Little Pincushions*, *Button! Button!*, and *Pretty Little Potholders*.

FANNIE NARTE lives in Texas, where she is a fiber and mixed-media artist pursuing her art degree. She is also a musician and entertainer who has performed with her husband and daughters in Hawaii, California, Louisiana, and Texas.

LOUISE PAPAS is one half of the Audrey and Maude pattern design team, and she has fun creating new designs for softies, aprons, and bags. She documents all these

crafty pursuits in her blog at www.lululollylegs.blogspot.com.

LISA M. PENNY has experimented in quilting, from precision piecing to free-form art quilts, as well as in mixed-media fiber collage and fabric/fiber sculpture. You can stroll through her online gallery at www.pennyfabricart.com.

LYNDA RAPP has been a neonatal intensive care nurse for 25 years. She loves her chosen profession, but she finds that sewing and crafting allow her an outlet for her creative juices. She showcases some of her work at www.sheffieldstudio.com.

AIMEE RAY is the author of *Doodle Stitching* (Lark Books, 2007), a collection of contemporary embroidery designs, and she has contributed to many other Lark Books titles. See more of her work at www.dreamfollow.com.

DORIE BLAISDELL SCHWARZ lives in a small Illinois community called Farmer City with her husband and their young daughter. She keeps a craft blog at www.tumblingblocks.net.

RUTH SINGER is a British textile designer-maker who creates bespoke and limited edition textiles and accessories using organic and vintage fabrics. Her book *Sew It Up* was published in 2008. Find out more at www.ruthsinger.com.

SARAH ANN SMITH is a regular columnist for *Machine Quilting Unlimited* magazine. She also teaches, has a line of patterns, and sells her work at www.sarahannsmith.com.

ANDI STERN'S work can be seen at her blog at www.andibeads.blogspot.com and at her website, www.embellishmentcafe.com.

SUSAN LEWIS STOREY lives in Austin, Texas. Her online portfolio is at www.susanstorey.com, and information about the classes she teaches can be found at www.intentionalarts.com.

CANDACE TODD fills her days with mothering, sewing, and searching for vintage treasures, and she posts all about it at www.candacetodd.blogspot.com.

acknowledgments

This book is a wonderful labor of love produced by a diverse group of craft artists and publishing professionals. The magic of the book starts with the very talented quilters who contributed their creativity and imagination to produce the beautiful mini-quilt projects. Thank you for sharing your fantastic designs.

Thanks also to the dedicated Lark Books staff. Assistant editor Beth Sweet helped shape the developmental process of the book, particularly in the selection of artists and quilt designs. Valerie Van Arsdale Shrader offered sage advice. Editor Larry Shea deftly moved the book through the production phase. The art direction of Megan Kirby and art production of Jeff Hamilton perfectly captured the series' pretty, fun aesthetic, complemented by the excellent work of photographers Steve Mann and Stewart O'Shields and illustrator Susan McBride. Finally, thanks to our outstanding cover designer Celia Naranjo, talented model Shelly Schmidt, and design-template creator Orrin Lundgren.

— **Ray Hemachandra,**
senior editor

index